Adolescent Development in the Family

Harold D. Grotevant, Catherine R. Cooper, *Editors*

A15041 885002

NEW DIRECTIONS FOR CHILD DEVELOPMENT

WILLIAM DAMON, *Editor-in-Chief*

Number 22, December 1983

Paperback sourcebooks in
The Jossey-Bass Social and Behavioral Sciences Series

Jossey-Bass Inc., Publishers
San Francisco • Washington • London

Harold D. Grotevant, Catherine R. Cooper (Eds.).
Adolescent Development in the Family.
New Directions for Child Development, no. 22.
San Francisco: Jossey-Bass, 1983.

New Directions for Child Development Series
William Damon, *Editor-in-Chief*

New Directions for Child Development (publication number
USPS 494-090) is published quarterly by Jossey-Bass Inc., Publishers.
Second-class postage rates are paid at San Francisco, California,
and at additional mailing offices.

Correspondence:
Subscriptions, single-issue orders, change of address notices,
undelivered copies, and other correspondence should be sent to
New Directions Subscriptions, Jossey-Bass Inc., Publishers,
433 California Street, San Francisco, California 94104.

Editorial correspondence should be sent to the Editor-in-Chief,
William Damon, Department of Psychology, Clark University,
Worcester, Massachusetts 01610.

Library of Congress Catalogue Card Number LC 83-82344
International Standard Serial Number ISSN 0195-2269
International Standard Book Number ISBN 87589-934-X

Cover art by Willi Baum
Manufactured in the United States of America

Ordering Information

The paperback sourcebooks listed below are published quarterly and can be ordered either by subscription or single-copy.

Subscriptions cost $35.00 per year for institutions, agencies, and libraries. Individuals can subscribe at the special rate of $21.00 per year *if payment is by personal check*. (Note that the full rate of $35.00 applies if payment is by institutional check, even if the subscription is designated for an individual.) Standing orders are accepted. Subscriptions normally begin with the first of the four sourcebooks in the current publication year of the series. When ordering, please indicate if you prefer your subscription to begin with the first issue of the *coming* year.

Single copies are available at $7.95 when payment accompanies order, and *all single-copy orders under $25.00 must include payment*. (California, New Jersey, New York, and Washington, D.C., residents please include appropriate sales tax.) For billed orders, cost per copy is $7.95 plus postage and handling. (Prices subject to change without notice.)

Bulk orders (ten or more copies) of any individual sourcebook are available at the following discounted prices: 10–49 copies, $7.15 each; 50–100 copies, $6.35 each; over 100 copies, *inquire*. Sales tax and postage and handling charges apply as for single copy orders.

To ensure correct and prompt delivery, all orders must give either the *name of an individual* or an *official purchase order number*. Please submit your order as follows:

Subscriptions: specify series and year subscription is to begin.
Single Copies: specify sourcebook code (such as, CD8) and first two words of title.

Mail orders for United States and Possessions, Latin America, Canada, Japan, Australia, and New Zealand to:
Jossey-Bass Inc., Publishers
433 California Street
San Francisco, California 94104

Mail orders for all other parts of the world to:
Jossey-Bass Limited
28 Banner Street
London EC1Y 8QE

New Directions for Child Development Series
William Damon, *Editor-in-Chief*

CD1 *Social Cognition,* William Damon
CD2 *Moral Development,* William Damon
CD3 *Early Symbolization,* Howard Gardner, Dennie Wolf
CD4 *Social Interaction and Communication During Infancy,* Ina C. Uzgiris
CD5 *Intellectual Development Beyond Childhood,* Deanna Kuhn
CD6 *Fact, Fiction, and Fantasy in Childhood,* Ellen Winner, Howard Gardner

CD7 *Clinical-Developmental Psychology,* Robert L. Selman, Regina Yando

CD8 *Anthropological Perspectives on Child Development,* Charles M. Super, Sara Harkness

CD9 *Children's Play,* Kenneth H. Rubin

CD10 *Children's Memory,* Marion Perlmutter

CD11 *Developmental Perspectives on Child Maltreatment,* Ross Rizley, Dante Cicchetti

CD12 *Cognitive Development,* Kurt W. Fischer

CD13 *Viewing Children Through Television,* Hope Kelly, Howard Gardner

CD14 *Childrens' Conceptions of Health, Illness, and Bodily Functions,* Roger Bibace, Mary E. Walsh

CD15 *Children's Conceptions of Spatial Relationships,* Robert Cohen

CD16 *Emotional Development,* Dante Cicchetti, Petra Hesse

CD17 *Developmental Approaches to Giftedness and Creativity,* David Henry Feldman

CD18 *Children's Planning Strategies,* David Forbes, Mark T. Greenberg

CD19 *Children and Divorce,* Lawrence A. Kurdek

CD20 *Child Development and International Development: Research-Policy Interfaces,* Daniel A. Wagner

CD21 *Levels and Transitions in Children's Development,* Kurt W. Fischer

Contents

Editors' Notes   1
Harold D. Grotevant, Catherine R. Cooper

Chapter 1. Adolescent Ego Development and Family Interaction: 5
A Structural-Developmental Perspective
Sally I. Powers, Stuart T. Hauser, Joseph M. Schwartz,
Gil G. Noam, Alan M. Jacobson
Patterns of communication differ between families of adolescents with advances
and families of adolescents with arrests in ego development. Relying on a model
of structural-development psychology, this study examines how adolescent ego
development is enhanced by exposure to different points of view and by opportunities to take the role of others and to share one's own perspective.

Chapter 2. Parental Validation and Support in the Development   27
of Adolescent Daughters
David C. Bell, Linda G. Bell
Qualities of the family system and parental behaviors mediate between parents'
personal resources, such as ego development and self-regard, and the adolescent's development of similar personal resources. Analyses of family communication processes and of self-perceptions of family functioning suggest that validation and support can predict patterns of development in adolescent females.

Chapter 3. Individuality and Connectedness in the Family as a   43
Context for Adolescent Identity Formation and Role-Taking Skill
Catherine R. Cooper, Harold D. Grotevant, Sherri M. Condon
The family is a context in which the adolescent attains a sense of identity, which
includes formulating a cohesive set of personal values and beliefs, and mature
role-taking skill, which involves developing the ability to differentiate and coordinate different points of view. This study examines family communication in
terms of both individuality and connectedness of family members.

Chapter 4. Young Adults and Their Parents: 61
Individuation to Mutuality
Kathleen M. White, Joseph C. Speisman, Daryl Costos
Analysis of young adults' views of their relationships with parents, including
current family interactions, differences of opinion, advice giving and care-
giving, reveals a progression from initial separation to attainment of peer-like
mutuality that relates to the young adult's development and marital status.

Chapter 5. Family Paradigm and Adolescent Social Behavior   77
David Reiss, Mary Ellen Oliveri, Karen Curd

The concept of family paradigm—the set of core assumptions that a family holds about its environment—is useful for considering the relationships between adolescence and family process from two vantage points: the relation between families' beliefs about the world and the patterns of engagement in it shown by their adolescents, and the adolescents' individual qualities of empathy.

Chapter 6. Social Construction of Adolescence by Adolescents   93
and Parents
James Youniss

This chapter discusses points of congruence and divergence raised by the five preceding chapters. Adolescent development in the family is seen as a transformation, not as a dismantling, of the parent-child relationship that endures throughout the overlapping life spans of parents and their adult children. The author integrates this view with current work in sociology and social history that emphasizes the processes by which the individual's sustained involvement in relationships with family and friends becomes the context for development of the self.

Index   111

Editors' Notes

Research efforts in several different disciplines concerned with the psychosocial development of adolescents are beginning to converge in their focus both on the role of relationships in the development of the individual, and on the contribution of that development to the quality of the individual's relationships. These efforts are being conducted by a cohort of investigators in such diverse disciplines as developmental psychology, psychiatry, family therapy, and sociology in an attempt to understand the interface between several aspects of adolescent psychosocial development and family relationships in which the adolescent participates. The chapters in this volume highlight findings from several of these efforts.

The goal of this volume is to bring into focus both the similarities and the differences among these investigations in order to enhance the cumulative nature of research evidence emerging in this area. The first five chapters describe studies being conducted by five different teams, each with its own theoretical approach and distinctive constructs and methodologies. The final chapter integrates results from the research reports and places them in perspective within the social sciences. To guide the reader, we will outline five themes that raise common issues addressed by these investigations. For each theme, we pose questions that may provide some perspective on what the studies can tell us as well as on what we have yet to learn.

The studies described in this volume cover a period in the life span from early adolescence to young adulthood. Thus, each study has had to address the distinctive transition or challenge faced by the young person at that developmental level. Two studies—that by Powers, Hauser, Schwartz, Noam and Jacobson described in Chapter One and that by Reiss, Oliveri, and Curd described in Chapter Five—focus on the period of early adolescence, a time for renegotiation of the young person's role as child within the family and the concomitant adjustments that parents may or may not make. Two other studies—that by Bell and Bell described in Chapter Two and that by Cooper, Grotevant, and Condon described in Chapter Three—examine processes of family communication during late adolescence as the adolescent is being launched into the worlds of college or work. Finally, the project of White, Speisman, and Costos described in Chapter Four follows young adults longitudinally from age twenty-two to twenty-six in an attempt to validate a developmental sequence moving from autonomy to mutuality in relationships with parents. An important contribution made by these studies is that adolescence is not a single unitary phase of development but a larger time frame that encompasses several substages, each of which warrants examination.

In viewing these chapters from a developmental perspective, readers may wish to consider the following questions: What are the normative changes in family communication processes experienced between early adolescence and young adulthood? What effects does the timing of such events as puberty, leaving home, and marriage of children have on relationships in the family? What kinds of research designs best capture the interplay between the adolescent's individual development in such areas as identity formation, ego development, and role-taking skill, the timing of these life events, and family relationships?

A second issue that all five teams of investigators have had to confront concerns the direction of effects: How can sequential analysis techniques be applied to understand directions of influence within a conversation? What limits the drawing of conclusions about causality from structural equations models? What limits the use of linear analytic techniques, such as Pearson correlations, multiple regression, and path analysis, in the study of variables that may be related in curvilinear ways?

Another theme that unifies these studies is that they all confront the formidable theoretical challenges associated with the study of processes and relationships. Each study has gone beyond simple status variable comparisons, such as between intact and divorced families or between middle and lower socioeconomic statuses to examine the inner workings of the family. The construct of individuation plays a key role in three studies. White, Speisman, and Costos view individuation as an early stage in the transformation of the young adult's relationships vis-á-vis parents. Their study of relationships examines the young adult's journey from a position of autonomy, which they call *individuation,* to a more peer-like sense of mutuality with parents. Bell and Bell view individuation as a process in which partners validate each other's view of the world and in so doing promote the development of differentiated self-awareness for both. Cooper, Grotevant, and Condon consider individuation to be a characteristic of a relationship in which there is a balance or blend of individuality and connectedness. All three teams have had to grapple with the complex problems posed by describing potential developmental changes in the adolescent's relationships with important others, such as parents.

To the degree that these approaches are successful, one may ask how these concepts can be useful in conceptualizing other relationships, such as those between spouses, siblings, or peers. We may also ask what are the key dimensions by which parents and children negotiate changes in their relationships and how these dimensions differ from those associated with the traditional socialization literature, such as support and control.

Fourth, each team has been actively engaged in extending the methodological tools needed to reduce and analyze interactional and relational data. In all five chapters, the researchers have outlined their particular coding and data reduction schemes to show clearly how these proceed from their theoretical framework. Detailed information about particular coding schemes can be obtained from the authors. Here, the relevant questions include: What are the advantages of multiple coding systems in data reduction and analysis? What are the limitations? At what point does the diversity of coding schemes hamper integration of research findings?

Fifth, all the teams have attempted to highlight the experience of adolescents as members of families that are clarified by their distinctive approaches. In Chapter Five, Reiss, Oliveri, and Curd discuss the processes by which each family constructs its own sense of reality and the ways in which that shared family paradigm is exhibited in behavior. In Chapter Three, Cooper, Grotevant, and Condon contrast the decision-making styles of several families to show how family communication processes provide the context in which the adolescent's freedom to explore is shaped. In Chapter Four, White, Speisman, and Costos present compelling examples of young adults' perspectives on their parents to illustrate their sequence of development in family relationships. Considering the experience of adolescence raises a practical concern: How can the findings of these studies by translated for lay audiences? How can parents and adolescents benefit from the results?

We hope that this volume will stimulate others to investigate questions raised by the coconstruction of developing relationships across the life span. This view of individual development in an interpersonal context is becoming more evident in studies of infant development and the transition to parenthood. Examination of analogous issues in adolescence will illustrate the usefulness of this perspective for an age when multiple systems can be examined. We hope that the focus of this volume on processes of interaction will expand the scope of research on normal family relations beyond self-report methodologies. As Youniss observes in Chapter Six, the context of coconstruction of relationships can best be understood from observational work. Certainly, we have much to gain by examining these processes and comparing them with the more conventional dimensions of support and control examined in the literature on parental socialization. Finally, we hope that these chapters will serve as both example and invitation to continued interdisciplinary theoretical and empirical work on individual development in the context of the family.

Harold D. Grotevant
Catherine R. Cooper
Editors

Harold D. Grotevant is associate professor in the Department of Home Economics, Division of Child Development and Family Relationships, and in the Department of Psychology at the University of Texas at Austin. He is especially interested in the contribution of the family to adolescent identity formation and career development.

4

Catherine R. Cooper is associate professor in the Department of Home Economics, Division of Child Development and Family Relationships, and in the Department of Psychology at the University of Texas at Austin. Her research interests concern the role of communication in the development of relationships, both within the family and in peer groups.

For structural-developmental psychology to be useful in investigating the relationship between adolescent development and family interaction, its perspective must be expanded to include the role of affect and of cognitively inhibiting behaviors in producing environments for development.

Adolescent Ego Development and Family Interaction: A Structural-Developmental Perspective

Sally I. Powers, Stuart T. Hauser, Joseph M. Schwartz, Gil G. Noam, Alan M. Jacobson

The relationship between family interaction and the psychological functioning of individual family members has been a productive area of research for several decades. However, most of this research has attempted to associate specific family behaviors with children's psychiatric hospitalization, delinquency,

This work was supported by grants from the Maternal and Child Health Research Grant Program, the Spencer Foundation, the MacArthur Foundation, the American Diabetes Foundation, the Joslin Diabetes Center Biomedical Research Support Program and DRTC, and the National Institute of Mental Health (RSDA #5k-02-MH-70178) (Dr. Hauser). Stephanie Beukema, Kirk Daffner, Dena Grossier, Christine Huber, Eydie Kasendorf, Karen Liese, John Temple, and Barbara Turner assisted in data collection. Jennifer Johnson and Bob Putnam coded transcripts of family interactions. Erin Phelps provided valuable statistical consultation, and Jennifer Johnson contributed to data management and computer programming. Lawrence Kohlberg and William Beardslee provided helpful comments on a draft of this chapter.

H. D. Grotevant and C. R. Cooper (Eds.). *Adolescent Development in the Family.* New Directions for Child Development, no. 22. San Francisco: Jossey-Bass, December 1983.

6

or drug abuse, not to examine the relationship between family environments and variables of individual development. Moreover, few studies have examined the relationship between family process and personality development in adolescence longitudinally. The Adolescent and Family Development Study of Harvard Medical School is a longitudinal project designed to investigate adolescent personality development and familial influences on development. It has assessed moral development (Noam and Powers, 1982; Powers and others, 1983a, 1983b), adolescent defense mechanisms and other ego processes (Beardslee and others, 1983), self-esteem (Jacobson and others, 1981), self-image (Hauser and others, 1983a), and other aspects of family environments (Hauser and others, 1983b; Powers, 1982). This chapter describes our examination of the relationship between adolescent ego development and family interaction. Using data from the first wave of our study, we will address three major questions: How are family interactions associated with arrested, delayed, or advanced adolescent ego development? Is the relationship between ego development and family interaction different in families of psychiatrically ill adolescents and in families of adolescents with no psychiatric illness? Can structural-developmental psychology provide a useful guide for investigating the relationship between adolescent ego development and family interaction? We will describe a new family interaction assessment technique and present cross-sectional results from the first year of our longitudinal study. Our hypothesis about the relationship between family processess and adolescent ego development and our measures of developmental and family interaction variables are based on the structural-developmental perspective.

Ego Development

Several theoretical traditions offer different models and empirical approaches to the study of ego development. In the psychoanalytic framework, ego development usually refers to the development of a collection of related processes, including cognitive functions, defenses, and interpersonal skills. Systematic assessment of these processes has been difficult to achieve. In contrast, Loevinger and her associates (Loevinger and Wessler, 1970; Loevinger and others, 1970) have developed a reliable method of measuring ego development based on a view that the essence of the ego is the process of integrating and making sense of experience. Structural-developmental psychology is an important theoretical foundation of this model of ego development. (The theories of Harry Stack Sullivan (1953) are relevant to Loevinger's conception of ego development.) The structural-developmental approach first gained widespread recognition through its application to cognitive development (Piaget, 1967), but it has been used increasingly over the last two decades to understand and describe social and personality development (Kohlberg, 1969; Selman, 1976; Kegan, 1982). Building on the assumptions of the structural conception of development, Loevinger (1976) describes ego development as a hierarchically ordered, invariant sequence of stages in which the individual's perception of self, others, and interpersonal relations becomes increasingly more differentiated and complex. Each stage differs from the others along intrapsychic and interpersonal dimensions and is a qualitatively distinct way of understanding the social world. The stages are defined independently of age and are divided into three levels: preconformist, conformist, and postconformist. Individuals in the preconformist stages are wary and impulsive, and they have stereotyped cognitive styles and exploitative or dependent interpersonal styles. Individuals in the conformist stages are concerned with interpersonal acceptance and show an increase in self-awareness. Individuals in the postconformist stages cope with inner conflict through a high degree of self-awareness and cognitive complexity, and they emphasize mutuality, empathy, and acceptance of individual differences in their interpersonal relations. Table 1 summarizes Loevinger's model of ego development.

Most research on ego development has concentrated on describing the basic structure of each stage, gathering evidence for individual differences and hierarchical sequence, and assessing the relationship of ego development with other psychological processes and capacities. Very little empirical research has sought to discover the kinds of interactions between individuals and their families that stimulate or inhibit development or how an individual's behavior within the family reflects his or her level of ego development. The Adolescent and Family Development Study was designed to investigate these two issues.

Ego Development and Family Interaction: Theoretical Assumptions

The structural-developmental approach asserts that an individual actively constructs an organized, unified way of understanding the world that undergoes successive changes as a result of the individual's interactions with the social and physical environment. Social environments are particularly important for stimulating or interfering with ego development, because the ego is a structure of expectations about interpersonal phenomena (Loevinger, 1976). In order to stimulate development, the social environment must challenge the child's current way of understanding the social world. "As long as the child is operating in an environment that does not conform to his expectations and that disconfirms them in a way to pace his growth, he has the potential for further growth" (Loevinger, 1976, p. 311). These disconfirming experiences produce cognitive conflict and cause children to change their way of viewing the world in an effort to interpret new experiences. Cognitive conflict about interpersonal relations can often be produced by encouraging a child to take the role of others and see that others reason and value differently. This process of role taking requires that similarities and differences in people's perspectives be clearly communicated. Our study investigates the assumption that development is stimulated by environments that challenge a child's current way of

Table 1. Milestones of Ego Development

Stage	Impulse Control "Moral" Style	Interpersonal Style	Conscious Preoccupations	Cognitive Style
Preconformist				
Presocial (1-1)		Autistic	Self vs. nonself	
Symbiotic (1-1)		Symbiotic	Self vs. nonself	
Impulsive (1-1)	Impulsive, fear	Receiving dependent, exploitive	Bodily feelings, especially sexual and agressive	Stereotypy, conceptual confusion
Self-protectiveΔ	Fear of being caught, externalizing blame, opportunistic	Wary, manipulative, exploitive	Self-protection, wishes, things, advantages, control	
Transition from self-protective to conformist (Δ/3)	Obedience and conformity to social norms are simple and absolute rules	Manipulative, obedient	Concrete aspects of traditional sex roles, physical causation as opposed to psychological causation	Conceptual simplicity, stereotypes
Conformist				
Conformist (1-3)	Conformity to external rules, shame, guilt for breaking rules	Belonging, helping, superficial niceness	Appearance, social acceptability, banal feelings, behavior	Conceptual simplicity, stereotypes, clichés
Transition from conformist to conscientious; self-consciousness (1-¾)	Dawning realization of standards, contingencies, self-criticism	Being helpful, deepened interest in interpersonal relations	Consciousness of the self as separate from the group, recognition of psychological causation	Awareness of individual differences in attitudes, interests and abilities, mentioned in global broad terms

Postconformist

Conscientious (1-4)	Self-evaluated standards, self-criticism	Intensive, responsible, mutual, concern for communication	Differentiated feelings, motives for behavior, self-respect, achievement traits, expression	Conceptual complexity, idea of patterning
Transition from conscientious to autonomous	Individuality, coping with inner conflict	Cherishing of interpersonal relations	Communicating, expressing ideas and feelings, process and change	Toleration for paradox and contradiction
Autonomous (1-5)	Add: Coping with conflicting inner needs	Add: Respect for autonomy	Vividly conveyed feelings, integration of physiological and psychological causation of behavior, development, role conception, self-fulfillment, self in social context	Increased conceptual complexity; complex patterns, toleration for ambiguity, broad scope, objectivity
Integrated (1-6)	Add: Reconciling inner conflicts, renunciation of unattainable	Add: Cherishing of individuality	Add: Identity	

Source: Hauser, 1976.

Note: Table 1 is reprinted from the *Psychological Bulletin* (1976, *83*, 928–955) by permission of the publisher and author. Copyright 1976, American Psychological Association. This table was originally adapted from Loevinger and Wessler, 1970.

understanding interpersonal relationships by providing opportunities to take the role of others through clear communication of differences and similarities of viewpoints. In addition, we examine the hypothesis that development can be delayed by family environments that are cognitively inhibiting and that thus interfere with sustained communication.

Although structural-developmental psychology has stressed the importance of cognitively stimulating environments for ego development, it has neglected to define the role of affect in producing environments that are beneficial or harmful to development. We hypothesize that cognitively stimulating interactions within the family are not sufficient for growth: For children to attend to the cognitively stimulating behaviors of parents, those behaviors must be accompanied by an atmosphere of positive affect and support. A supportive climate allows family members to feel safe enough to challenge one another's ideas. Cognitive challenges that are given in a nonsupportive context can be interpreted as criticism and arouse defensiveness, which discourages the exploration necessary for new understanding and growth. Thus, family behaviors indicative of affective conflict should be negatively associated with adolescent ego development.

The influence of social environments on ego development has been investigated by school intervention studies (Blasi, 1972; Erickson, 1974). However, these studies have not directly observed or documented the actual social interactions assumed to stimulate development, and they have not investigated interactions that could be hypothesized to impede development. Moreover, the intervention studies did not examine the role of affect in ego development empirically, and they did not study the impact of families on development. The Adolescent and Family Development Study addresses all these issues by investigating the association of cognitively stimulating behaviors, cognitively inhibiting behaviors, supportive affect, and affective conflict within the family and adolescent ego development. It also assesses the relationship between the adolescent's own behavior within the family and the adolescent's level of ego development. Although Loevinger's model of ego development does not predict a relationship between ego development and specific behaviors, her descriptions of the different character styles evident at each stage suggest that one could find general behavior patterns linked to ego stage (Hauser, 1976, 1978).

Method

Sample. The sample of fifty-nine upper- and middle-class adolescents and their parents consisted of two groups: nonpatient suburban high school students ($N = 32$, eighteen girls and fourteen boys) and psychiatrically hospitalized adolescents ($N = 27$, fourteen girls and thirteen boys). The psychiatric sample was drawn from a population of successive admissions to the adolescent unit of a private psychiatric hospital. All patients diagnosed as having thought disorder or organic brain damage were excluded from the sample. The majority of the adolescent patients' diagnoses fell into two categories listed in the *Diagnostic and Statistical Manual of Mental Disorders* (American Psychiatric Association, 1980), adjustment disorder and conduct disorder. The high school students were selected from 230 freshman volunteers attending a suburban high school by matching these students for sex and age with the psychiatric sample. The fifty-nine adolescents and their families were selected from our study's larger sample of psychiatrically hospitalized adolescents and high school students by including all adolescents with two parents living at home. The age of the adolescents ranged between twelve and sixteen; 85 percent of the adolescents were fourteen or fifteen years old, and the mean age of adolescents in both groups was 14.5 years. Group differences in the relationship of family interaction with ego development were investigated to illuminate the role of the family in both the normal and the delayed course of ego development and adolescent psychopathology.

Procedures. For the nonpatient family subjects, the family interaction sessions took place in the adolescent's high school. For families of adolescent patients, the family sessions were held at the psychiatric hospital where the adolescent was a patient. Strodtbeck's (1958) revealed differences procedure was used to generate the family interactions. Each parent and adolescent individually responded to Form A of Kohlberg's Moral Judgment Interview (Colby and others, in press), which asks the subject how best to solve three moral dilemmas. Family members were then brought together, and the differences in their solutions to these dilemmas were revealed. Family members were asked to explain their individual positions and to attempt to reach a consensus that would represent the entire family. The experimenter was not present for this interaction. Each family discussed at least three differences so as to include all three possible coalitions (father and child versus mother; mother and child versus father; mother and father versus child).

All family discussions were audiotaped in order to preserve interruptions, simultaneous speech, and other paralinguistic cues, such as hesitation, laughter, and stuttering. The tapes were transcribed, and the typed transcripts, divided into units according to the presence of certain key events in the interaction, became the data base for the interaction analyses. Since our aim was to study how families deal with the discussion behaviors of their adolescent child and how their responses affect the child, the key event that we used for unitizing family discussions was any intelligible speech expressed by the adolescent in the discussion. We also developed rules specifying a consistent amount of speeches surrounding each adolescent speech within the unit. All the speeches contained in these units were numbered consecutively and given at least one code. A speech was defined as all the words spoken by a single speaker from the time when he or she started to speak to the time when he or she stopped. Interrater reliability for unitizing the transcripts ranged from 75 to 85 percent exact agreement between three unitizers for twenty transcript

12

pages. Interrater reliability for number of speeches ranged from 84 to 98 percent exact agreement.

Assessments. The Developmental Environments Coding System (DECS) (Powers, 1982) codes interaction variables assumed by structural-developmental psychology to affect ego development and other constructs, such as moral judgment. The DECS assesses twenty-four different kinds of family behaviors that are indicative of cognitively stimulating behaviors, cognitively inhibiting behaviors, and affective support and conflict. These twenty-four behaviors are grouped into eight conceptually derived summary categories: focusing, competitive challenging, noncompetitive sharing of perspectives, support, avoidance, rejection of the task, distortion, and affective conflict. The DECS coding manual defines each code conceptually, discusses important distinctions between codes, and provides multiple examples for each code. Codes assess the function of each speech in the discussion, not the level of verbal, cognitive, or affective complexity of the individual speeches.

Four summary categories are hypothesized to stimulate ego development, while four categories are hypothesized to interfere with ego development (see Table 2). That is, the categories of focusing, competitive challenging, noncompetitive sharing of perspectives, and support are hypothesized as stimulating to ego development. Focusing behaviors draw attention to differences and similarities in family members' perspectives and check for clear understanding of one another's viewpoints. Competitively challenging behaviors critique another person's position or defend one's own perspective. Noncompetitive sharing of perspectives includes behaviors that clarify one's own opinion or request clarification of another's opinion. These three categories contain behaviors assumed to provide cognitive stimulation by providing clear communication of different ways of understanding the social world. (Many of the codes in these three categories adapt codes developed by Berkowitz and Gibbs (1979, in press) to code verbal behaviors in college students' dialogues.) The behaviors in the category of support indicate positive affect and serve to encourage participation in family discussion.

Table 2. Developmental Environments Coding System Categories

	Cognitive Categories	Affective Categories
Stimulating to Development	Focusing Competitive challenging Noncompetitive sharing of perspectives	Support
Interfering with Development	Avoidance Distortion Rejection of the task	Affective conflict

The categories of avoidance, rejection of the task, distortion, and affective conflict are hypothesized as inhibiting to ego development. In order to promote role taking and (cognitive conflict) family members must be able to tolerate sharing and discussion of differences. The category of avoidance identifies behaviors that distract from the problem that the family is trying to discuss. Codes for rejection of the task identify speeches that show a refusal to do the task or an attempt to close the discussion before differences have been explored. Although rejection can be viewed as a type of avoidance, it appears to be a much stronger statement of intolerance of differences than simple distracting behavior. A code for distortion is given if a speaker gives a blatantly inaccurate representation of another discussant's view or incorrectly perceives the nature of the task. The categories of avoidance, rejection of the task, and distortion contain behaviors assumed to be cognitively inhibiting, because these behaviors interfere with sustained and coherent discussion of different perspectives. Codes in the category of affective conflict identify speeches that are markedly hostile attempts to attack another family member's personality or reasoning, sarcastic remarks, belligerent attempts at self-defense, attempts to undermine or devalue another person, threats of punishment or misbehavior, and attempts to block the participation of another person.

Interaction scores for each category were computed for each individual family member and for the total family. Because the total number of codes given to a discussion varied, interaction scores for each person and family were standardized by using the ratio of the frequency of codes given in a particular category to the frequency of total codes given. All speeches in all units contained within the entire transcript were coded.

To determine interrater reliability for the categories of the DECS, three raters coded each speech for every family member for eleven separate family discussions. These eleven discussions consisted of 2,178 coded responses. All raters were blind to the group assignment of the family, sex of the child, and ego stage of all family members. Pearson product-moment correlations, percent of agreement, and the kappa statistic were obtained for each pair of raters. Correlations ranged from .85 to .98, with an average of .94. Percent agreement ranged from .84 to .98 with an average of .94. Kappa ranged from .63 to .73, with an average of .69. All kappa scores were judged to be substantial using Landis and Koch's (1977) scale for interpreting the limits of acceptable kappa results in interrater reliability. Accurate estimations of kappa could not be obtained for the categories of avoidance and distortion because the frequency of speeches representing these categories was too low. Since the percent agreement of these categories was high and the appearance of these behaviors was deemed very important, we retained them in the coding system with the plan to conduct additional reliability analyses of these codes.

In addition to coding each speech according to the eight categories just described, every speech was also given a code for content, mode, level of transactiveness, who said the speech, to whom it was spoken, and to whom the speech referred. These codes and analysis using them have been described by Powers (1982).

Ego development for adolescents and parents was assessed by the Washington University Sentence Completion Test and accompanying scoring manual (Loevinger and Wessler, 1970; Loevinger and others, 1970). There is considerable evidence of favorable reliability and validity for this instrument (Hauser, 1976; Holt, 1980; Loevinger, 1979). An ordinal ego stage score and an interval score (item sum score) were derived from each thirty-six-item protocol. The item sum score is used for the correlational analyses reported in this chapter. Interrater reliability was computed by the intraclass correlation coefficient and was in the range of .70 to .80 for three coders. The coders were blind to the patient status, age and sex of the subjects, and the hypotheses of the study.

Socioeconomic status (SES) of both mothers and fathers was assessed by the Duncan Socioeconomic Index (Duncan, 1961). Each parent's level of education was measured with the Hollingshead Educational Scale (Hollingshead, 1957).

Results and Discussion

Background Variables. The SES of both mothers and fathers of psychiatric patients was significantly lower than that of mothers and fathers of nonpatient adolescents (mothers: $t = 3.22$, $p = .01$; fathers: $t = .04$, $p = .001$). Moreover, the SES of mothers was significantly lower than that of fathers in both groups (nonpatient group: $t = 3.28$; $p = .01$; patient group: $t = 2.90$, $p = .01$) and in the total sample ($t = 4.38$, $p = .0001$). The educational level of both mothers and fathers of psychiatric patients was significantly lower than that of mothers and fathers of nonpatient adolescents (mothers: $t = 5.84$; $p = .001$; fathers: $t = 6.26$, $p = .001$). The educational level of mothers was significantly lower than that of fathers both in families with no patients ($t = 5.02$) $p = .0001$) and in the total sample ($t = 4.17$, $p = .0001$). Because these variables correlated significantly with parental and adolescent ego development in the total sample, SES and education were controlled through multiple regression techniques in all analyses of the combined groups and in comparisons of mother and father ego scores. These background variables were not controlled in within-group analyses of the relationship between family interaction and ego development, because these variables did not correlate significantly with adolescent ego scores in either group.

Family Members' Ego Development. Fifty-three percent of the mothers in the total sample scored at the postconformist level, 43 percent scored at the conformist level, and 4 percent scored at the preconformist level. The distribution of ego scores was much the same for fathers: Fifty-five percent of the fathers scored at the postconformist level, 40 percent scored at the conformist level, and 5 percent scored at the preconformist level. There was no significant difference between the scores of mothers and fathers or between the scores of parents of patient and nonpatient adolescents when the parents' SES and education were controlled through multiple regression techniques.

However, very significant differences in ego development were obtained for the two groups of adolescents, even after parental SES and education were controlled. When group status was added as a variable in a hierarchical multiple regression equation after variables of parental SES and education, change in R^2 was .1589 ($F = 19.15$, $p \leq .0001$). The majority of nonpatient adolescents (53 percent) was at the conformist level of ego development, with the remaining adolescents in this group evenly divided between preconformist and postconformist stages. In contrast, 85 percent of the patient adolescents were preconformist, 11 percent were conformist, and 4 percent were postconformist. There were no significant differences in ego scores between adolescent girls and boys in either group.

The finding of very significant differences in the ego development of patient and nonpatient adolescents is even more striking when it is contrasted with the finding of no significant group differences in parents' ego development. Adolescent ego development cannot be accounted for by differences in parental ego development. This is underscored by the additional funding that there was no significant correlation between the ego stage of male or female adolescents and the ego stage of their mother or father in either group, even when parental SES and education were not controlled. These findings indicate the importance of investigating whether differences in patterns of family interaction are much more powerful predictors of adolescent ego development than parents' level of ego development. The structural-developmental perspective suggests that the strongest impact of the family on individual development comes through family interaction that encourages family members to understand one another's viewpoints actively, not through direct transmission of parental ego level to children by such mechanisms as identification, internalization, or imitation.

Adolescent Ego Development and Parental Behavior. The relationship between adolescent ego development and each category of parental behaviors was examined within each group and for the total sample of families. The most striking finding in both groups and in the total sample was that adolescent ego development was strongly and positively associated with the association of adolescent ego development with any of the cognitively stimulating behaviors shown by parents. In the total sample, mothers' and fathers' support was positively correlated with adolescent ego development (mother: $r = .45$, $p = .004$; father: $r = .47$, $p = .0002$). The positive relationship of mothers' and fathers' support to adolescent ego development remained when parents' SES and educational level were controlled through hierarchical multiple regression (mothers' support: change in $R^2 = .098$, $F = 10.28$, $p \leq .002$; fathers' support: change in $R^2 = .117$, $F = 12.79$, $p \leq .0008$). Nonpatient adolescents' ego development was positively correlated with support both from their mother ($r = .54$,

$p = .001$) and father ($r = .48$, $p = .006$). In families of psychiatrically hospitalized adolescents, only father's support ($r = .38$, $p = .04$) correlated with adolescent ego development. In contrast to these findings, none of the categories of parental behavior hypothesized to be cognitively stimulating (competitive challenging, noncompetitive sharing of perspectives, and focusing) was positively correlated with adolescent ego development. In fact, mothers' competitive challenging behaviors were negatively correlated with adolescent ego development in the nonpatient group ($r = -.36$, $p = .04$).

These results suggest that hypotheses that assume a positive linear relationship between cognitively stimulating interactions and development are too simplistic. Analysis of the relationship between ego development and combinations of different behaviors or interaction patterns may be much more informative. For example, although competitive challenging behaviors are hypothesized to stimulate development, it may be crucial to know what other kinds of interactions occur with and provide context for challenging statements. The presence of other kinds of behavior, especially affect-laden behaviors, may change the meaning and impact of challenging statements. The response to challenging statements may be very different if they occur in a context of affective conflict or in a context of support. The negative correlation of mothers' competitive challenging behaviors with adolescent ego development in the nonpatient group is less surprising when the mothers' challenging behavior is viewed in relation to other behaviors occurring with it. Correlations between mothers' challenging behaviors and other behaviors revealed that mothers of nonpatient adolescents who challenged did not give support ($r = -.55$, $p = .001$) and did not noncompetitively share their perspective ($r = -.89$, $p = .001$). In addition, mothers' affective conflict was significantly correlated with mothers' challenging ($r = .42$, $p = .02$).

Hierarchical cluster analysis (Johnson, 1967) was used to examine further the relationship of total behavior patterns to adolescent ego development. This analysis grouped families with similar interaction patterns into clusters. Interaction patterns were determined by the relative relationship of the eight behavior categories to one another within each family. Cluster analysis revealed seven clusters or patterns of family interaction in the total sample. Table 3 shows the rank in each behavior category and mean adolescent ego score for each cluster. Cluster analysis revealed that adolescent ego development was most advanced when families presented a high amount of noncompetitive sharing of perspectives or challenging behavior within a context of high support or a context of low affective conflict and cognitively inhibiting behavior. The cluster of families with the highest mean adolescent ego score showed at least 40 percent more supportive behavior than any other cluster, and it had the second highest amount of noncompetitive sharing of perspectives. In addition, the families in this cluster showed very little avoidance and distortion and the smallest amount of rejection or affective conflict of any cluster.

Table 3. Mean Adolescent Ego Stage and Rank in Each Behavior Category for Each Cluster

Cluster	N	Mean Adolescent Ego Stage	Mean Adolescent Item Sum Score	Behavior Categories							
				Focus	Challenge	Share	Support	Avoid	Reject	Distort	Affective Conflict
1.	11	3/4	164	5	4	2	1[a]	4.5	7	6	7
2.	6	3	150	6	1	7	5.5	6	5	5	3
3.	12	Δ/3	146	7	2	6	3	2	4	3.5	2
4.	14	Δ/3	141	4	3	4	5.5	4.5	6	3.5	5
5.	3	Δ/3	137	3	7	1	4	1	3	7	6
6.	12	Δ/3	128	2	5	3	2	3	2	2	4
7.	1	2	111	1	6	5	7	7	1	1	1

[a] Rank 1 signifies that families in this cluster had the highest score given for this behavior catetory.

The family interaction pattern typical of the cluster of families with the highest mean adolescent ego score can be illustrated by the interaction of one adolescent, Sharon, and her parents. Sharon's family did not shy away from discussing their differences in opinion; however, their explanations of their differences were not competitive and did not arouse defensive responses. When Sharon's parents disagreed with her, they earnestly tried to clarify their own way of viewing the problem. It was clear that Sharon listened to these explanations; at the same time she felt very free to expound on her own way of reasoning. Sharon's parents took pride in her struggle to think for herself. Although her mother disagreed with her, she stated, "Sharon is so reasonable with her decision. She's a reasonable person." Her father underlined this support of Sharon by saying, "You're working very hard with these ideas!" Because the family did not construe the task as a competitive one in which someone must win and someone must lose, the family agreed to disagree about how to solve the moral dilemma. Sharon's father stated, "I'm sitting here rather happy that Sharon has a feeling about this dilemma that she has, and I'm willing to let that sit." This family decision to disagree was not a rejection or avoidance of the task, because the decision was reached after careful deliberation and discussion of the family's differences and similarities in opinion.

The importance of examining the relationship between adolescent ego development and combinations of different types of behaviors can be illustrated by a comparison between the cluster just described and another cluster. Families in the second cluster also exhibited a high amount of noncompetitive sharing of perspectives, but they combined this sharing with a high amount of avoidance. Although families in this cluster shared their opinions, they quickly began to distract from the task of discussion. Their avoidance behaviors seemed to signify that family members were not able to tolerate exploring their differences long enough to grapple actively with understanding one another's views. By avoiding the discussion, they escaped cognitive or affective conflict. This type of family interaction pattern may represent a kind of pseudomutuality (Wynne and others, 1968). The mean ego score of adolescents in this cluster was much lower (preconformist) than it was for adolescents in the first cluster.

Like noncompetitive sharing of perspectives, the association of competitive challenging behaviors with ego development appears to be much more positive when the context of these behaviors is taken into account. The cluster with the second highest mean adolescent ego score (conformist level) had the highest amount of competitive challenging behavior of any cluster and low amounts of avoidance, rejection, and distortion. The importance of context is evident when this cluster is compared with a different cluster in which families combined high amounts of avoidance with challenging behaviors. Adolescents in the second cluster scored at the preconventional level of ego development.

The two clusters with the lowest mean adolescent ego scores exhibited the highest amounts of focusing, rejection of the task, distortion, and affective conflict. This interaction pattern can be illustrated by the discussion of Jimmy and his parents. Soon after each family member had stated his or her opinion, Jimmy's father asked, "Jimmy, you're just in a hurry to finish, right?" Jimmy responded, "I'm not in a hurry, I just don't like arguing." Jimmy viewed the discussion of differing opinions as arguing and tried to close the discussion as soon as possible. The following interchange between Jimmy and his parents illustrates Jimmy's reasons for fearing a situation in which family members must voice their differences. In this interchange, Jimmy begins by stating a clear opinion: He agrees with his mother that parents should be honest with their children. Jimmy's father immediately challenges his statement with a series of questions that tend to put Jimmy in the wrong, regardless of how he answers. Jimmy's responses become more and more tentative until he finally decides that the only safe answer is to stop the discussion.

Mother: I think it's important for a parent to be honest with their child. 'Cause I remember whenever my mother answered me, she always told me the truth.

Father: Well, I don't know about that.

Jimmy: I agree with you, Mom.

Father: You're gonna tell your kids the truth all the time?

Jimmy: No, not all the time.

Father: What are you gonna tell them, a lie?

Jimmy: I'll tell them the truth, but in a way they can understand it.

Father: Yeah, but do you think we've been truthful to you for the most of your life?

Jimmy: I hope so.

Father: Well, do you think so?

Jimmy: I don't know.

Father: Have we ever lied to you?

Jimmy: I don't know. I don't keep track of you, you don't keep track of me. So, we agree on the answer? Are we finished?

Father: Well, we wanted to develop it a little bit more, that's why.

Jimmy: I don't want to develop it.

Father: You just want to get out of here and play ping pong, right?

Jimmy: No, I don't want to develop it, all right?

Father: Why?

Jimmy: Because I don't.

Father: But that's part of the study. That's what we're here for.

Jimmy: I don't care. I don't want to. We developed it enough. We all agree on it. We all agree families should be open and everything.

Father: Okay. I guess that's about it then, right?

In discussing another question, Jimmy's mother does not allow him to clarify his own opinion. She tells him: "That's not the right way to feel." She then distorts Jimmy's viewpoint by stating what she thinks Jimmy really feels:

"I think you wouldn't want to tell. You'd hate to tell, but you know you'd have to, because you really care about your duty. I know you, and I know you'd tell." Although his mother will not listen to Jimmy's own statement of his view, she objects when he tries to concede to her. Jimmy finally gives in and states: "all right, I'll tell on him." His mother replies: "You can't feel that way. You can't say, 'Oh well, if you say so, I'll tell.' You have to have your own opinion." All family members decide to stop the discussion at this point, although Jimmy has not been allowed clearly to state his own agreement or disagreement with his parents' viewpoint.

The interaction patterns exhibited by families in this cluster also indicated that families need to focus the discussion overtly only when unusual amounts of distortion are present. Although we hypothesized that focusing behaviors stimulated adolescent development, the highest amounts of focusing behaviors appeared among families in the clusters with the highest distortion scores.

Adolescent Ego Development and Adolescent Behavior. Finding meaningful associations between an adolescent's ego development and the adolescent's behavior would lend support to the thesis that an adolescent's level of ego development directly influences his or her family's interaction patterns. Our findings reveal that low levels of adolescent ego development are reflected in both cognitively and affectively inhibiting adolescent behavior. Nonpatient adolescents' ego development was positively related to their use of support ($r = .45$, $p = .01$). Adolescent patients' ego development was negatively related to their rejection of the task ($r = -.33$, $p = .09$) and affective conflict ($r = -.35$, $p = .06$). Adolescent ego development in the total sample was negatively associated with adolescent rejection of the task ($4 = -.56$, $p = .0001$). When adolescent ego score was added as a variable in a hierarchical multiple regression equation after variables of parental SES and education, change in R^2 was .097 ($F = 10.19$, $p = .002$).

Conclusions

In this chapter, we have described a methodology for studying the relationship between family environment and adolescent ego development, and we have presented findings based on data collected during the first year of our longitudinal study. Both the results and our methods suggest new directions for the study of adolescent development within the context of the family.

Our findings emphasize the importance of investigating the effects of parental behavior on adolescent development. Parental ego development is not directly related to the level of adolescent ego development. The only other investigation of the relationship between parental and child ego development that we know about—the study by Bell and Bell described in Chapter Two— reports the same result. Our emphasis on parental behavior, not on such mechanisms as identification or internalization, is in accord with the structural model of development.

Investigations of the relationship between family interaction and adolescent development should include direct observation and assessment of family behaviors. Our results suggest that the Developmental Environments Coding System provides a theoretically based method that can reliably identify family interactions that are associated with variations in adolescent ego development.

The role that affect plays in producing family environments that are beneficial or detrimental to adolescent ego development must be examined. In our study, the amount of supportive interactions that parents gave during family discussions proved to be a very good predictor of adolescent ego development. The impact of affective interactions, such as support, on ego development has not previously been studied, presumably because the crucial quality of the environment that structural-developmental psychology has assumed to foster development is its ability to provide cognitive stimulation. Our study suggests that affect can have a direct influence upon ego development and that it also can serve as a mediating context by influencing the effect of cognitively stimulating behaviors on development.

Family behaviors that interfere with development and behaviors that facilitate development should both be investigated. In our study, family interaction patterns associated with low adolescent ego development exhibited the highest amounts of cognitively inhibiting behaviors and affective conflict.

Instead of simply focusing on the one-to-one association of discrete behaviors with developmental level, we should examine the overall interactive context in which a particular behavior is exhibited when we investigate the relationship between behavior and development. In our study, the relationship between parents' cognitively stimulating behaviors and adolescent ego development seems to depend on the interactive context in which the cognitive stimulation is given. Cluster analysis revealed that adolescents from families with the highest amounts of sharing of perspective given in a context of support had the highest ego development and that adolescents in families with the highest amount of challenging had the second most advanced ego development. When sharing of perspectives or challenging was combined with high amounts of cognitively inhibiting behaviors or affective conflict, adolescent ego development was much lower. If the interactive context determines the impact of a sharing or challenging statement, then analyses that fail to take this context into account may not find a relationship between cognitive stimulation and adolescent ego development.

Our results point to the need for further examination of how a structural-developmental approach to ego development can contribute to an understanding of adolescent psychopathology. Nonpatient high school students had significantly higher levels of ego development than psychiatrically hospitalized adolescents. The majority of patients was at the preconformist level of development. One essential feature of many patients' diagnosis was "a repetitive and persistent pattern of conduct in which either the basic rights of others or major age-appropriate societal norms or rules are violated" (American Psychiatric Association, 1980, p. 35). This description can be compared with Loevinger's (1976) description of preconformist reasoning. At the preconformist level, rules are followed only if they are backed by punishment or when it is to the individual's immediate interest. Individuals at this level do not consider the interests of others, they do not recognize that others' interests can differ from their own, or they believe that, if different interests do exist, everyone is responsible for ensuring that his or her own needs are satisfied. There is no perspective of shared needs and no attempt to live up to the expectations of others. Other people are valued for what they can give. Thus, persons at this level can seem demanding, dependent, and manipulative. If an adolescent remains at the preconformist level, his or her reasoning and consequent behavior may be seen as progressively age-inappropriate, and he or she becomes more likely to be labeled as deviant.

Our results also indicate group differences in the relationship between family behaviors and adolescent ego development. Mothers' support was not associated with patients' ego development although it was highly correlated with nonpatients' development. In addition, patients' development was negatively associated with their own expression of affective conflict, while there was no significant association between the developmental level of nonpatient adolescents and affective conflict.

Longitudinal analyses are crucial for determining how adolescent development can change the ways in which the family interacts and how family interaction can influence the course of individual development. Although our study indicates that there are some strong associations between family behaviors and adolescent ego development, we cannot assume that these behaviors cause adolescent development. An equally valid explanation of our findings is that parents are more likely to respond with cognitively stimulating and supportive behaviors to an adolescent with an advanced level of ego development than they are to an adolescent with a low level of ego development. By making repeated observations of family interaction and individual ego development, our study intends to distinguish long-standing family interactions that precede shifts in the adolescent's development from family patterns that emerge subsequent to developmental changes in the adolescent.

Longitudinal analyses can shed light on another important issue concerning the relationship between family behavior and individual development: Do different family interaction patterns provide stimulation for different points in an individual's development? Although the interactions that structural-developmental psychology postulates as stimulating to development have been assumed to benefit individuals at all levels, some interactions may be especially crucial for particular stage transitions. Our finding that parental support is positively associated with adolescent ego development may be related to our having studied early adolescents. Early adolescents are often making the transition from preconformist to conformist reasoning. This transition necessitates identification with a group and broadening of one's understanding of personal relationships. If parental support strengthens the child's understanding of the value both of being a member of group and of maintaining interpersonal relationships, it may thus facilitate the transition from preconformist to conformist reasoning. Our longitudinal data on the ego development and family interactions of adolescents and parents will allow us to investigate whether different patterns of family interaction become more important at different stage transitions. Our analyses may also illuminate the ways in which social environments that facilitate adult development differ from social environments that benefit adolescent development.

In subsequent reports, we will examine the longitudinal patterns of family interaction and development as well as explore the influence of parent-to-parent interactions on adolescent and parent ego development, sex differences in the relationship between developmental level and family environments and individual behavior, and the association of patterns of family interactions with other measures of adolescent development.

References

American Psychiatric Association. *Diagnostic and Statistical Manual of Mental Disorders.* (3rd ed.) Washington, D.C.: American Psychiatric Association, 1980.

Beardslee, W., Jacobson, A., Hauser, S., Noam, G., and Powers, S. "An Approach to Evaluating Adolescent Ego Capacities." Unpublished manuscript, 1983.

Berkowitz, M. W., and Gibbs, J. C. "A Preliminary Manual for Coding Transactive Features of Dyadic Discussion." Unpublished manuscript, Marquette University, 1979.

Berkowitz, M. W., and Gibbs, J. C. "Measuring the Developmental Features of Moral Discussion." *Merrill-Palmer Quarterly,* in press.

Blasi, A. "A Developmental Approach to Responsibility Training." Unpublished doctoral dissertation, Washington University, 1972.

Colby, A., Kohlberg, L., Gibbs, J. C., Candee, D., Hewer, A., Power, C., and Speicher-Dubin, B. *Measurement of Moral Judgment: Standard Issue Scoring Manual.* New York: Cambridge University Press, in press.

Duncan, O. D. "A Socioeconomic Index for All Occupations." In A. J. Reiss (Ed.), *Occupations and Social Status.* New York: Free Press, 1961.

Erickson, L. V. "Psychological Growth for Women: A Cognitive-Developmental Curriculum Intervention." *Counseling and Values,* 1974, *18* (2), 102–116.

Hauser, S. T., "Loevinger's Model and Measure of Ego Development: A Critical Review." *Psychological Bulletin,* 1976, *83,* 928–955.

Hauser, S. "Ego Development and Interpersonal Style in Adolescence." *Journal of Youth and Adolescence,* 1978, *1,* 333–352.

Hauser, S., Jacobson, A., Noam, G., and Powers, S. "Ego Development and Self-Image Complexity in Early Adolescence: Longitudinal Studies of Psychiatric and Diabetic Patients." *Archives of General Psychiatry,* 1983a, *40,* 325–332.

Hauser, S. T., Powers, S. I., Noam, G. G., Jacobson, A. M., Weiss, B., and Follansbee, D. J. "Familial Contexts of Adolescent Ego Development." *Child Development,* 1983b.

Hauser, S., Powers, S., Jacobson, A., and Noam, G. *Working with Adolescents: Ego Development and Family Processes.* New York: Free Press, forthcoming.

Hollingshead, A. B. *Two-Factor Index of Social Position.* New Haven: Yale University Press, 1957.

24

Holt, R. R. "Loevinger's Measure of Ego Development: Reliability and National Norms for Male and Female Short Forms." *Journal of Personality and Social Psychology*, 1980, *39*, 909–920.

Jacobson, A., Hauser, S., Powers, S., and Noam, G. "The Impact of Diabetes on Adolescent Psychological Development." In S. Laron and A. Galatzer (Eds.), *Psychosocial Aspects of Diabetes in Children and Adolescents*. Basel: Karger, 1981.

Johnson, S. C. "Hierarchical Clustering Schemes." *Psychometrika*, 1967, *32*, 241–254.

Kegan, R. *The Evolving Self.* Cambridge, Mass.: Harvard University Press, 1982.

Kohlberg, L. "Stage and Sequence: The Cognitive Developmental Approach to Socialization." In D. A. Goslin (Ed.), *Handbook of Socialization Theory and Research.* Chicago: Rand McNally, 1969.

Landis, J. R., and Koch, G. C. "The Measurement of Observer Agreement for Categorical Data." *Biometrics*, 1977, *33*, 159–174.

Loevinger, J. *Ego Development: Conceptions and Theories.* San Francisco: Jossey-Bass, 1976.

Loevinger, J. "Construct Validity of the Sentence Completion Test of Ego Development." *Applied Psychological Measurement*, 1979, *3*, 281–311.

Loevinger, J., and Wessler, R. *Measuring Ego Development.* Vol. 1: *Construction and Use of a Sentence Completion Test.* San Francisco: Jossey-Bass, 1970.

Loevinger, J., Wessler, R., and Redmore, C. *Measuring Ego Development.* Vol. 2: *Scoring Manual for Women and Girls.* San Francisco: Jossey-Bass, 1970.

Noam, G., Powers, S., Hauser, S., and Jacobson, A. "Adolescent Ego Development and Moral Development in Psychiatric Patients and Normal Controls." In L. Kohlberg and D. Candee (Eds.), *Research in Moral Development.* Cambridge, Mass.: Harvard University Press, forthcoming.

Piaget, J. *Six Psychological Studies.* New York: Vintage Books, 1967.

Powers, S. I. "Family Interaction and Parental Moral Development as a Context for Adolescent Moral Development." Unpublished doctoral dissertation, Harvard University, 1982.

Powers, S., Hauser, S., Noam, G., and Jacobson, A. "Adolescent Moral Development and Family Interaction." In L. Kohlberg and D. Candee (Eds.), *Research in Moral Development.* Cambridge, Mass.: Harvard University Press, 1983a.

Powers, S., Noam, G., Hauser, S., and Jacobson, A. "The Relationship of Parental Ego and Moral Development: A Longitudinal Study." In L. Kohlberg and D. Candee (Eds.), *Research in Moral Development.* Cambridge, Mass.: Harvard University Press, 1983b.

Selman, R. L. "Social-Cognitive Understanding: A Guide to Educational and Clinical Practice." In T. Lickona (Ed.), *Moral Development and Behavior.* New York: Holt, Rinehart and Winston, 1976.

Strodtbeck, F. L. "Husband-Wife Interaction over Revealed Differences." *American Sociological Review*, 1958, *16*, 468–473.

Sullivan, H. S. *The Interpersonal Theory of Psychiatry.* New York: Norton, 1953.

Wynne, L. C., Ryckoff, I. M., Day, J., and Hirsch, S. I. "Pseudomutuality in the Family Relations of Schizophrenics." *Journal of Psychiatry*, 1968, *21*, 205–220.

Sally I. Powers is an instructor in the Department of Psychiatry, Harvard Medical School, associate director of the Adolescent and Family Development Study at Massachusetts Mental Health Center, and research associate at the Henry A. Murray Research Center of Radcliffe College.

Stuart T. Hauser is associate professor of psychiatry at Harvard Medical School, director of the Adolescent and Family Development Study, and a psychiatrist at McLean Hospital, Belmont, Massachusetts.

Joseph M. Schwartz is an assistant psychologist at McLean Hospital, where he directs a halfway house for emotionally disturbed adolescents. He is an instructor in the Department of Psychiatry, Harvard Medical School and a special candidate in psychoanalysis, Boston Psychoanalytic Society and Institute.

Gil G. Noam is a clinical and developmental psychologist, a lecturer at Harvard Medical School, associate director of the Adolescent and Family Development Study at McLean Hospital, and codirector of the Clinical-Developmental Institute, Belmont, Massachusetts.

Alan M. Jacobson is assistant professor of psychiatry at Harvard Medical School, associate director of the Adolescent and Family Development Study, and Chief of Psychiatry at the Joslin Diabetes Center, Boston.

*An individuation process involving validation and a valuing
process involving support act as mediating processes between
parent development and adolescent development.*

Parental Validation and Support in the Development of Adolescent Daughters

David C. Bell
Linda G. Bell

Texts on adolescent psychology leave one with the impression that the major
function of the family during this developmental phase is to give the adolescent
someone to leave. The emphasis is on breaking ties and establishing independence from parents and on unrealistic parental expectations that parents can
still have influence on their offspring. Although it has long been recognized
that the family provides a primary environment for socialization, the major
focus of research on this issue has been families with young children. This traditional approach is now being broadened in two ways. On the one hand,
researchers are becoming increasingly aware of adolescence as part of a con-
tinuum of development and of the importance of the family in adolescence.
On the other hand, a paradigm shift that conceptualizes individual behavior as
constrained by and nested in ongoing systems of relationships of which the
family is the primary representative seems to be emerging.

This research is supported by a grant from the National Institute of Mental
Health (RO3 MH28190). The authors thank Connie S. Cornwell for her careful eval-
uation of the theoretical model. The authors' contributions are equal; names are listed
in alphabetical order.

H. D. Grotevant and C. R. Cooper (Eds.). *Adolescent Development in the Family.* New
Directions for Child Development, no. 22. San Francisco: Jossey-Bass, December 1983.

The family has always been seen as an instrument for the transmission of values and skills from parents to children. The family systems perspective views each family member's behavior as both contributing to and constrained by an ongoing family pattern. Characteristics of the family system include shared values, such as a general comfort with conflict and confrontation, or the valuing of individual achievement. Other characteristics include patterns that call for one person to be labeled as different (the angry one, the bad one, the star) in order for the pattern to be maintained.

From a family perspective, it is the pattern that is relatively constant, whereas particular individual behavior is to some degree interchangeable. For example, if family members believe that the continuing survival and evolution of the family requires one person to be depressed (so that the others can deny their own sadness) or a child to be labeled as a disciplinary problem (so that the husband and wife can cope with marital stress), the person who assumes the role can change over time. When one person speaks to avert conflict, this action can be on behalf of the family: A function is performed that another family member would otherwise have to perform. Thus, from a family systems perspective, analysis of ongoing family interaction gives information about the level of support or comfort with disagreement within the family, but it says less about the attitudes and values of individual family members.

Many paths connect family system processes and the individual development of family members. Family interactions involve close relationships in which personal resources, such as self-esteem and competence, affect each individual's attitudes and perceptions of others, which in turn affect interpersonal behavior. Interpersonal behavior then affects the maintenance and development of personal resources. The family is a primary interpersonal environment in that the styles of perceiving and relating to others throughout life can be patterned here.

In this chapter, we will examine parental characteristics as determinants of the family system climate. We view the family climate as affecting the ways in which parents relate to an adolescent daughter during a family discussion of disagreements. We view qualities of the family system and parental behaviors as mediators between the parents' personal resources, such as ego development and self-regard, and the adolescent's development of similar personal resources. Although our research focuses on the adolescent's development as an end product of the family system, we feel that it is important to recognize that both children and parents contribute to the creation and maintenance of the system and that the individual functioning and development of all family members are affected by the family system.

The Individuation Process

An important link between the individual and the family system is expressed in the individuation process (Bell and Bell, 1979, 1982a, 1982b).

Our model of this process has been greatly influenced by the work of Boszor-menyi-Nagy (1965), Bowen (1971, 1976), Laing (1965), Minuchin (1974), Skynner (1976), and Wynne and others (1958). The individuation process, which is depicted in Figure 1, relates differentiated self-awareness to openness to others, accurate interpersonal perception, and mutual validation among family members. Differentiated self-awareness refers to a person's self-concept, which realistically differentiates and incorporates the various aspects of the personality. We operationalize this concept by using Loevinger's (1966) measure of ego development.

Differentiated self-awareness influences the perception of others by at least two routes. First, as one's self-awareness increases, so does one's aware-ness of the complexities of others' personalities. This in turn makes one more open to others and induces one to be more attentive to them and to evaluate the accuracy of one's expectations about them. Second, the more self-aware individual is also likely to be more self-accepting. Thus, the self-aware individ-

Figure 1. The Individuation Process

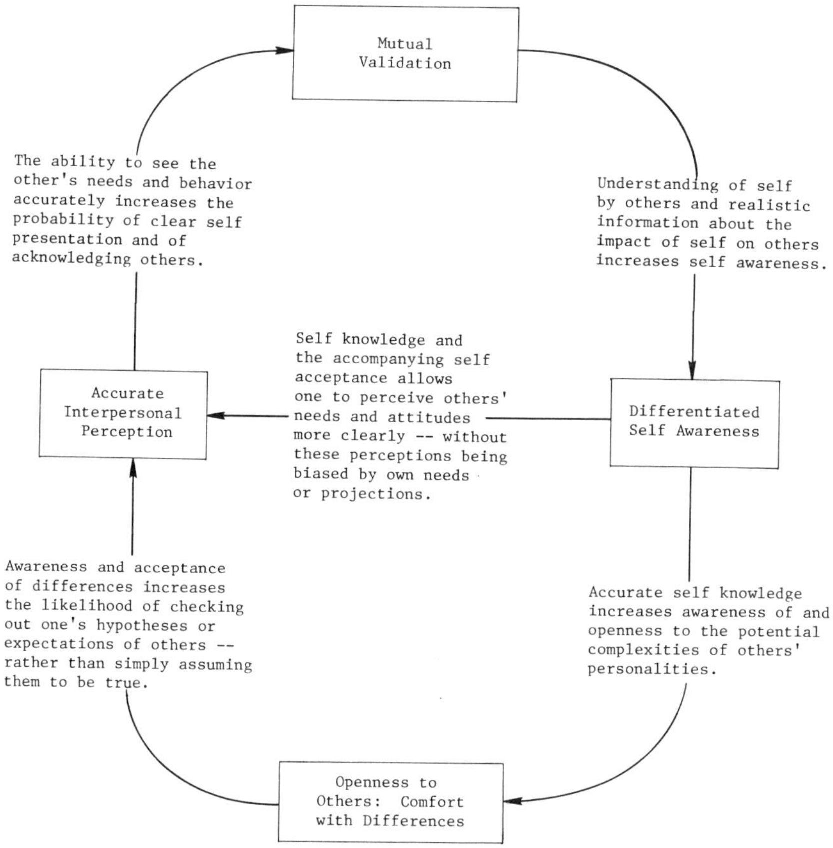

ual is less likely to attribute particular inaccurate characteristics to others as a way of bolstering his or her own sense of security. For example, a person who feels weak and vulnerable can misperceive an equally weak mate as strong.

Accuracy of interpersonal perception enhances individuals' ability to carry on a mutually validating relationship and to communicate: "I heard what you said; what you are saying makes sense to me." Validation also involves responding to the other, in effect saying, "What you are doing and saying has a specific effect on me; here is how I react." Accurate perception of the other enhances one's ability to present oneself effectively. Likewise, one's ability to provide the other with understanding and to meet the other's needs depends on one's ability to receive the other's communication accurately and to perceive the other's needs accurately. Thus, increased accuracy of interpersonal perception increases mutual validation. Mutual validation increases each individual's self-awareness, because the information received from the other is accurate.

The same cycle can be described negatively. To the extent that one's understanding of the complexities of one's own personality is incomplete, one's view of others will tend to be simplistic. Other people's actions will be hard to understand, and one will be reluctant to deal with others' complexities. This selective inattention makes one an inaccurate observer. Moreover, an individual who is unable to acknowledge or accept important aspects of the self is more likely to experience a biased perception of others; strong personal needs lead to a lack of attention or to selective attention to others' behavior, which prevents one from responding clearly and appropriately to the other's needs and from providing the other with accurate information about oneself. Failure to receive an appropriate response is disappointing. Mutual invalidation and mutual misunderstanding give one unreliable information about one's effects on others and thus prevent one from increasing one's self-awareness.

The Valuing Process

In earlier analyses of the individuation process, we found that parental characteristics associated with people's taking responsibility for themselves and not for others were different from those associated with a warm, supportive environment. Thus, the one pattern was consistent with the individuation process. The other pattern led us to conceptualize the valuing process.

The valuing process, which is depicted in Figure 2, relates positive self-regard of individual family members to their ability to support one another. Positive self-regard increases one's openness to others in one's interpersonal environment as one generalizes one's self-regard to positive expectations about others. These positive expectations lead one to be positive and receptive toward others. Openness and receptivity toward others in turn leads one to show warmth and support in one's interactions with them. Support is a matter of showing positive regard to others, in effect saying "I like you." Mutual sup-

Figure 2. The Valuing Process

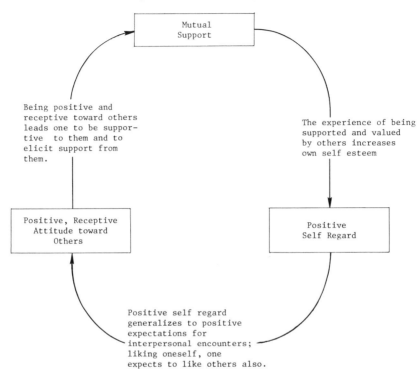

Mutual
Support

Being positive and
receptive toward others
leads one to be suppor-
tive to them and to
elicit support from
them.

The experience of being
supported and valued
by others increases
own self esteem

Positive, Receptive
Attitude toward
Others

Positive
Self Regard

Positive self regard
generalizes to positive
expectations for
interpersonal encounters;
liking oneself, one
expects to like others also.

port and the accompanying experience of being valued by the other enhances one's own self-esteem.

While the individuation process focuses on the development of accurate self- and other awareness through mutually validating relationships, the valuing process focuses on the development of positive self-regard through positive supportive relationships. We underline the difference between our conceptualizations of validation and support. This difference derives in part from the work of others who have coded the family interaction process microanalytically (Mishler and Waxler, 1968; Riskin and Faunce, 1969). Validation is based on an awareness of and comfort with individuality and differences. This awareness allows family members to listen to one another without prejudice or expectations based on their own needs. Family members can respond to one another in an acknowledging and clear way. People receive accurate feedback about how others in the family perceive and respond to them. This does not mean that they necessarily agree with one another or even that they like each other. In contrast, support refers to positive regard or liking. It is quite possible for a family to be supportive and invalidating at the same time. In such families, people are uncomfortable with disagreements and have few conflict resolution skills.

Theoretical Model and Method

The structural model that we tested in preparing this chapter is depicted in Figure 3. It draws heavily on our understanding of both the individuation and the valuing process. In this model, the parents' personal development is taken as a precursor of the family climate. Parental behavior toward the daughter is seen as deriving from the family climate and as instrumental in the development of differentiated self-awareness and positive self-regard by an adolescent daughter in the family. The two processes are connected through the concept of comfort with differences, which is expected to be associated both with accurate interpersonal perception among family members and with a family climate of warmth and support, because comfort with differences not only leads one to be able to see others accurately but also encourages one to be open and receptive to them.

Families of 100 adolescent girls participated in a structured two-hour interview in their home. These families represent a normal population; they were selected with the cooperation of local high schools in a large midwestern city. The sample represents a homogeneous population of white, middle-class, two- and three-child families, each with a fifteen- to seventeen-year old girl. Two hundred eighty-three girls agreed to participate in a session in which they completed shortened forms of Loevinger's sentence completion measure of ego development (Loevinger, 1966; Loevinger and Wessler, 1970) and of the California Psychological Inventory (CPI). Those who had very high Good Impression or very low Communality scores on the CPI were excluded as well as those whose parents were both foreign-born and those whose families had severe health problems. Of 215 eligible girls, 100 girls and their families agreed to be interviewed.

During the home interview, each family member completed a shortened form of the Moos Family Environment Scale (Moos, 1974), which focuses on such issues as family cohesiveness, conflict, organization, and expression of feelings. Here are some typical true-false items: "Family members really help and support one another." "We fight a lot in our family." "Family members are rarely ordered around." "We say anything we want to around home." Later, the family participated in a revealed difference exercise based on their answers to the questionnaire. They discussed approximately ten items on which they had disagreed, and they tried to reach agreement. Items were selected to reflect a variety of topics as well as a variety of coalitions within the family. Family interaction during this discussion was audio tape-recorded. The transcript of this discussion provided the data for microanalytic and global coding. During the home interview, parents and children completed other instruments, including Loevinger's ego development for the parents and a brief questionnaire developed by Feldman (1975) that includes a measure of positive self-regard.

Two kinds of coding were done on the family transcripts, one involving microanalytic phrase-by-phrase coding, the other a rating by clinically sophis-

Figure 3. Individuation and Valuing Processes, Showing Operational Measures

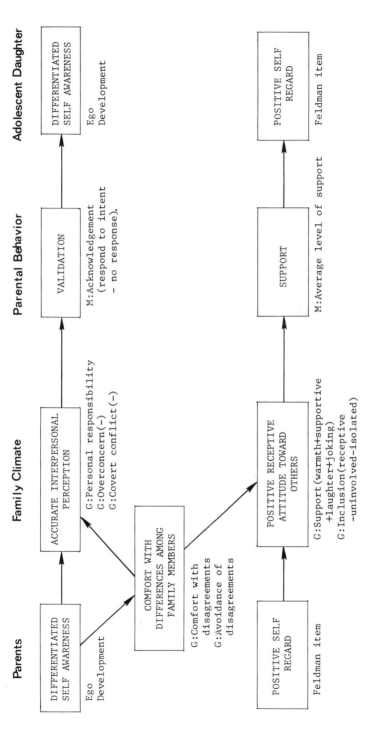

Parents	Family Climate	Parental Behavior	Adolescent Daughter

DIFFERENTIATED SELF AWARENESS
Ego Development

ACCURATE INTERPERSONAL PERCEPTION
G:Personal responsibility
G:Overconcern(-)
G:Covert conflict(-)

VALIDATION
M:Acknowledgement (respond to intent – no response).

DIFFERENTIATED SELF AWARENESS
Ego Development

COMFORT WITH DIFFERENCES AMONG FAMILY MEMBERS
G:Comfort with disagreements
G:Avoidance of disagreements

POSITIVE RECEPTIVE ATTITUDE TOWARD OTHERS
G:Support(warmth+supportive +laughter+joking)
G:Inclusion(receptive –uninvolved–isolated)

SUPPORT
M:Average level of support

POSITIVE SELF REGARD
Feldman item

POSITIVE SELF REGARD
Feldman item

Note: "G" indicates items from the Global scale; "M" indicates codes from the microanalytic Interaction Process Coding Scheme. (See text for further descriptions.)

ticated coders on a group of global scales. The microanalytic coding used two scales from the Interaction Process Coding Scheme (Bell and others, 1982). The Support scale describes the quality of the affective relationship between family members. The tone of voice and the content of each unit of speech were coded on a seven-point scale ranging from very supportive (warm, accepting) to very nonsupportive (defensive, rejecting). Support is considered to be movement toward the other, such as reinforcing, encouraging, or caring for the other. Nonsupport shows movement away from the other, such as disapproving, excluding, criticizing, attacking, or rebuking the other. The Acknowledgment scale codes people's responses to each other as responsive to intent, focus, or both; not responsive; or explicitly invalidating. Examples of acknowledgment coding are given in Table 1.

The Global scales (Bell and Cornwell, 1982) were used by graduate students in family therapy to code a number of dimensions, including clarity of expression of ideas, ability to acknowledge differences, comfort with disagreement, quality of affect (sadness, anger, warmth), and expression of feelings. The operational variables used to measure each variable in Figure 3 are as follows: For each family member, Differentiated Self-Awareness (Loevinger's ego development) and Positive Self-Regard (self-rating of "the way you feel about yourself," Feldman, 1975), were assessed.

Three Family Climate measures were derived from Global Scales ratings of family discussion: Accurate Interpersonal Perception, Comfort with Differences, and Positive Receptive Attitude. While we have no direct measures of perception, we can measure behaviors that reflect the accuracy of interpersonal perception. These measures focus on individuals' taking responsibility for themselves rather than for others and on the degree of covert con-

Table 1. Examples of Acknowledgement Codes

Question: "Do we have privacy at home?"

1. Response to intent	"Yes."
2. Response to intent and focus	"Yes, we do have privacy."
3. Response to focus	"Privacy at home is a big issue."
4. Recognition	"Hmm. Our home is a big place."
5. No response	"Susie is at Sam's."
6. Explicit invalidation	"That's a stupid question."

Statement: "I think the answer is true."

1. Response to intent	"I disagree."
2. Response to intent and focus	"I agree the answer is true."
3. Response to focus	"The answer could be anything."
4. Recognition	"Well, uh."
5. No response	"You look sad."
6. Explicit invalidation	"You're nuts, it's false."

Source: Bell and others, 1982.

flict in the family. When individuals see each other clearly and accurately, acceptance of differences occurs. Thus, accuracy of interpersonal perception can be inferred when family members take personal responsibility for their own thoughts, feelings, and behaviors and when family members are neither overly concerned with nor overly reactive to each other. In this climate, individuals feel comfortable expressing themselves, with few hidden agendas and little covert conflict.

Accurate Interpersonal Perception was indexed by personal responsibility — family members take responsibility for their own actions, feelings, and thoughts, not for those of others; overconcern — the family atmosphere is overly close and members are "stuck" or overly concerned with each other (a negative measure reflecting inaccurate interpersonal perception); and degree of covert conflict in the family (a negative measure). Comfort with Differences was indexed by comfort with differences or disagreements and avoidance of disagreements, which combines two scales: Family seems to avoid differences and disagreements, and family members withdraw from the task because it seems threatening. (Scales were combined to facilitate analysis of the structural model by limiting the number of observable variables and the number of parameters that had to be estimated). Positive Receptive Attitude was indexed by support — a combination of four scales: amount of warmth, support, warm laughter, and joking — and inclusion — a combination of three scales: family members are open and receptive to statements made by others, are less involved in the task because people are excluded (a negative measure), and seem isolated, disconnected, and apathetic toward each other (a negative measure).

Parental behavior (measures from microanalytic coding) was indexed by two measures: validation of adolescent daughter used the Acknowledgment scale to code the times during the family discussion when each parent directly responded to the daughter. The measure was the percent of times when the parent responded to the intent of her statement (for example, by saying that he or she agreed or disagreed with the statement or by answering a question; coded 1 or 2 in Table 1) minus the percent of times when the parent made no response or was explicitly invalidating (codes 5 or 6 in Table 1). Support for Adolescent Daughter indexed the average of support when each parent was addressing the daughter.

Results

The theoretical model representing the individuation and valuing processes (see Figure 3) is estimated as a structural equation model using LISREL (Jöreskog and Sorbom, 1981). LISREL estimates the strength of causal relations most likely to have produced the observed correlations. LISREL has the advantage over simple path analysis and other forms of multiple regression analysis of allowing multiple indicators of some or all theoretical variables.

All relations indicated in Figure 3 were tested. In addition, each relation between a variable in the model and all subsequent variables (those to the right in Figure 3) were estimated. The results of the test are displayed in Figure 4. The initial full model and the final restricted model of Figure 4 differ by a chi-square of 34.42 based on thirty-eight degrees of freedom. All effects in Figure 4 have t-values greater than ± 2. Because of missing data on some variables, the analysis is based on seventy-eight cases. In the initial full model, no more than seventy-eight parameters can be estimated reliably. Thus, the effects of comfort with differences on parental behaviors and adolescent characteristics have been omitted. Because of the strong associations between husband and wife behaviors (.22 for validation, .71 for support), these relations are represented by reciprocal effects (for example, the effect of the husband's support for the adolescent on the wife's support and vice versa). In practice, because the mutual effects are not simultaneously identified, only one effect in each pair is actually estimated: wife's validation on husband's validation and husband's support on wife's support. The one selected in each pair is the one with the stronger independent effect. In general, the data support individuation and valuing as distinct processes relating family climate and individual development.

The Individuation Process. We predicted that the effect of parental ego development on adolescent ego development is mediated by a family climate of accurate interpersonal perception and parental validation of the daughter. Two direct effects of parents' ego development can be expected: First, parental ego development affects accuracy of interpersonal perception. Second, parental ego development affects comfort with difference, which in turn affects accuracy of interpersonal perception.

We found support for the first hypothesis: Both husbands' and wives' ego development have a positive effect on accuracy of interpersonal perception. The second hypothesis received only partial support: Neither husbands' nor wives' ego development affects comfort with difference, but comfort with difference affects accuracy of interpersonal perception.

Accuracy of interpersonal perception seems not to affect parental validation. In fact, we find accuracy of perception to be negatively associated with wife's validation of the daughter and not at all related to husband's validation. Furthermore, husband's validation of the daughter is not related to daughter's level of ego development. However, wife's validation of daughter is related to daughter's ego development, as the model predicts. We also found a strong direct effect of accuracy of interpersonal perception on adolescent ego development. The importance of family climate as a mediator between parental and adolescent ego development is highlighted by the absence of a direct effect of parental ego development on adolescent ego development. These results can be summarized as follows:

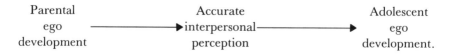

Figure 4. Final Model of Family Process: Individual Development Relationships

PARENTS   FAMILY CLIMATE   PARENTAL BEHAVIOR   ADOLESCENT

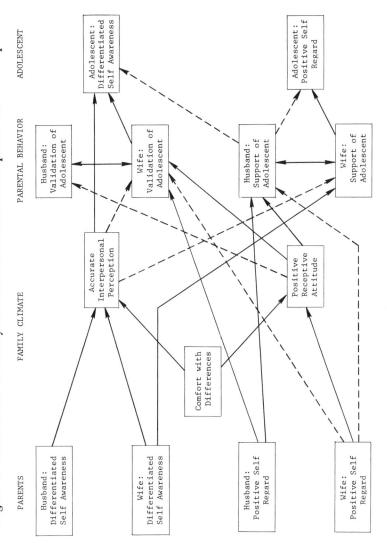

Note: Only those estimated effects with a *t*-value greater than ± 2.00 are shown. Positive effects are shown by solid lines; negative effects by broken lines. (See text for further discussion.)

These results uphold the hypothesis that the adolescent's ego development develops within a family process involving accurate interpersonal perception. Specifically, daughter's ego development is facilitated by a family system in which people take responsibility for themselves, in which people are not overly concerned with one another, and in which there is little covert conflict. This kind of family climate is facilitated by the parents' ego development and by the family's comfort with differences.

The Valuing Process. At first glance, the relationships among the variables associated with the valuing process may appear quite confusing. However, the picture can be clarified if we assume that two separate processes are occurring: The first is the predicted valuing process, while the second involves a quality of paternal support that is detrimental to the daughter.

The valuing process predicts that the effects of parental self-regard on adolescent self-regard are mediated by a receptive attitude in the family and by parental support of the adolescent daughter. General support for this process is found: Wife's positive self-regard is directly associated with a positive receptive attitude in the family. Both positive receptive attitude and husband's positive self-regard are directly related to husband's support of the adolescent daughter. Because of the strong association between husband's and wife's support, these variables also affect wife's support. The lack of a direct effect of positive receptive attitude on wife's support is at least in part an artifact of the strong effect of husband's support on wife's support. Thus, we can treat effects on the husband's support as if they were effects on the wife's support. Wife's support of the adolescent daughter is found to be positively related to daughter's positive self-regard. Finally, as in the case of the individuation process, there is no direct effect of parental characteristics (positive self-regard) on the same characteristic of the adolescent.

Our analyses indicate that husband's support has a negative effect on both daughter's ego development and daughter's level of positive self-regard. Although husband's positive self-regard is directly related to husband's support of his daughter, his wife's positive self-regard is negatively related to husband's support of his daughter. That is, the *lower* the wife's positive self-regard, the more the husband is involved in a supporting relationship with his daughter. A hypothesis that, we believe, explains these results is that the wife who has lower self-esteem is less likely to be involved in a supportive relationship with her husband. The husband turns to the daughter to make up for this lack of support, and the husband and the daughter become closer as a result.

However, father-daughter closeness in which the father seeks not to offer genuine support to the daughter but to meet his own needs can be detrimental to the daughter's development. Two other findings from our research support this interpretation. First, using perceptions of family climate to estimate coalitions within the family, Bell and Bell (1982b) found that adolescent girls who scored generally low on a number of personal development measures were more likely to be part of a family pattern in which there was a coalition between father and daughter that excluded the mother. Second, Bell and Eckman (1982) found that mothers involved in child abuse reported nonsupportive relationships with their own mothers but supportive relationships with their own fathers. Bell and Eckman speculated that this result was connected with an incestuous relationship between the wives and their fathers. However, the appearance of similar results in the current study of nonclinical (normal) families suggests that a more general process is at work.

Thus, we argue that the valuing process and the father-daughter support process should be distinguished. If this is done, the father-daughter support process can be depicted as follows:

Wife's   Husband's   Adolescent's
self- ----------------------► support for ----------------------► self-
regard   adolescent   regard

where the dashed lines indicate negative effects. If this process is removed from Figure 4, the remaining relationships generally confirm the predicted valuing process:

Parental   Positive   Parental   Adolescent
self- ------► receptive ------► support of ------► self-
regard   attitude   adolescent   regard.

This oversimplification of the results omits the direct effect of husband's self-regard on husband's support and shows husband's self-regard as affecting positive receptive attitude. However, this depiction reflects our belief that, when father-daughter negative support effect is removed, a positive effect of father's support remains.

Relationships Between Individuation and Valuing Processes. Our results support the importance of differentiating the individuation process from the valuing process. Parental ego development affects accurate interpersonal perception but not positive receptive attitude in the family climate. Likewise, accurate interpersonal perception affects the adolescent daughter's ego development but not her positive self-regard. However, the two processes are not totally independent. Comfort with differences between people helps to create a family climate that promotes receptive attitudes among family members and accurate interpersonal perception. The wife's ego development affects her support of her daughter. The husband's positive self-regard affects his wife's validation of their daughter.

There are also some negative connections. Accurate interpersonal perception is negatively related to wife's support, and positive receptive attitude is negatively related to husband's validation. So, while it is reasonable to expect that some family climates will reflect both accurate interpersonal perception and positive receptive attitudes, it is also conceivable that some families sense that these behaviors are incompatible. As a result, these families can feel that responding with clarity and directness reflects lack of support.

Discussion

Our study reflects the benefits of conceptualizing the family system as a mediator of the effects of parent personality on child development. There are no direct effects of parent ego development or self-regard on these same measures for the adolescent daughter. All effects are mediated through family climate variables and through specific parental behaviors. One of our most gratifying results is the linking of variables at different conceptual levels. The parents' individual characteristics affect the family climate, which in turn affects parental behavior and ultimately the adolescent daughter's personality.

Our data support the importance of both the individuation and the valuing process. The parents' level of ego development is transmitted to the adolescent daughter through a series of system and interactional variables (see Figure 1). Parental ego development and the family's comfort with difference affect the accuracy of interpersonal perception within the family. This in turn affects the daughter's ego development.

The valuing process is partially supported in these data. Wife's level of positive self-regard helps to create a family climate that promotes positive receptive attitudes among family members. This climate in turn is related to parents' support of the daughter. Wife's support for the daughter is positively related to daughter's positive self-regard.

The data indicate that the individuation and valuing processes are conceptually independent and empirically coherent. For example, accurate interpersonal perception is closely related to the ego development of individual family members but not to their degree of positive self-regard.

Perhaps the most unexpected findings of our study involve the negative relationships between paternal support and adolescent ego development and positive self-regard. Behaviors that have a positive impact for the wife and mother have a negative impact when performed by the husband and father. Our data show that an adolescent daughter's self-regard and self-awareness are positively related, respectively, to the mother's support and validation, but they are unrelated to the father's validation, and they are negatively related to his support.

Of course, these results about the effects of fathers are specific to the particular processes studied here. Data from earlier analyses (Bell and Bell, 1982c) support the positive impact of father's behavior on the adolescent daughter's development. Two paternal variables correlated positively both with the adolescent daughter's self-esteem and with her ego development: involvement, measured by the percent of speech that the father directed to the adolescent during the family discussion, and focus on the process of thinking, as reflected by such verbs as *understand, think, figure,* and *interpret.*

Mothers and fathers seem to affect an adolescent daughter's personality development in different ways. It is important to investigate both the constructive and the inhibiting processes commonly associated with each parent's role. It is even more important to understand each parent's behavior as part of the larger family pattern. For example, our data show that the father-daughter relationship cannot be described adequately without looking also at the husband-wife relationship.

Our results also suggest that future work on the impact of parents on adolescents can benefit from the family systems perspective; from differentiation of processes reflecting various aspects of the family-individual interface, including the individuation and valuing processes; and from openness to theorizing about and testing for differential aspects of the mother's and the father's role in relationship both to sons and to daughters.

References

Bell, D. C., and Bell, L. G. "Family Process and Child Development in Unlabeled (Normal) Families." *The Australian Journal of Family Therapy*, 1982a, *3*, 205–210.

Bell, D. C., Bell, L. G., and Cornwell, C. S. *Interaction Process Coding Scheme.* Houston: University of Houston, 1982. (Available from the authors.)

Bell, D. C., and Eckman, G. A. "The Dependency Process in Child Abuse." Paper presented at meetings of the American Sociological Association, 1982.

Bell, L. G., and Bell, D. C. "The Influence of Family Climate and Family Process on Child Development." Paper presented at meetings of the International Council of Psychologists, 1979. (ERIC Document ED 178 177)

Bell, L. G., and Bell, D. C. "Family Climate and the Role of the Female Adolescent: Determinants of Adolescent Functioning." *Family Relations,* 1982b, *31*, 519–527.

Bell, L. G., and Bell, D. C. "Parental Validation as a Mediator in Adolescent Development." Paper presented at meetings of the American Psychological Association, 1982c.

Bell, L. G., and Cornwell, C. *Global Scales.* Houston: University of Houston at Clear Lake City, 1982. (Available from the authors.)

Boszormenyi-Nagy, I. "A Theory of Relationships: Experience and Transaction." In I. Boszormenyi-Nagy and J. L. Framo (Eds.), *Intensive Family Therapy.* New York: Harper & Row, 1965.

Bowen, M. "Family Therapy and Family Group Therapy." In H. I. Kaplan and B. J. Sadock (Eds.), *Comprehensive Group Psychotherapy.* Baltimore: Williams & Wilkins, 1971.

Bowen, M. "Theory in the Practice of Psychotherapy." In P. J. Guerin (Ed.), *Family Therapy.* New York: Gardner Press, 1976.

Feldman, L. Unpublished research proposal. Chicago: The Family Institute of Chicago, 1975.

Jöreskog, K., and Sorbom, D. *LISREL: Analysis of Linear Structural Relationships by the Method of Maximum Likelihood (Version V).* Chicago: National Educational Resources, 1981.

Laing, R. L. "Mystification, Confusion, and Conflict." In I. Boszormenyi-Nagy and J. L. Framo (Eds.), *Intensive Family Therapy.* New York: Harper & Row, 1965.

Loevinger, J. "Meaning and Measurement of Ego Development." *American Psychologist,* 1966, *21*, 195–206.

Loevinger, J., and Wessler, R. *Measuring Ego Development.* Vol. 1: *Use of a Sentence Completion Test.* San Francisco: Jossey-Bass, 1970.

Minuchin, S. *Families and Family Therapy.* Cambridge, Mass.: Harvard University Press, 1974.
Mishler, E. G., and Waxler, N. E. *Interaction in Families.* New York: Wiley, 1968.
Moos, R. H. *Family Environment Scale.* Palo Alto: Consulting Psychologists Press, 1974.
Riskin, J., and Faunce, E. *Family Interaction Scales Scoring Manual.* Palo Alto: Mental Research Institute, 1969.
Skynner, A. C. R. *Systems of Family and Marital Psychotherapy.* New York: Brunner/ Mazel, 1976.
Wynne, L. C., Ryckoff, I. M., Day, J., and Hirsch, S. L. "Pseudomutuality in the Family Relations of Schizophrenics." *Psychiatry,* 1958, *21,* 205-220.

David C. Bell completed work on this chapter while an assistant professor at the University of Houston, Central Campus. His research interests include the study of interpersonal power processes through microanalytic analysis and the analysis of power processes in political and economic networks.

Linda G. Bell is an associate professor of behavioral science and Director of Training in Family Therapy at the University of Houston, Clear Lake City.

Observations of family communication indicate that adolescents who exhibit greater degrees of identity exploration and role-taking skill participate in relationships in which both individuality and connectedness are expressed.

Individuality and Connectedness in the Family as a Context for Adolescent Identity Formation and Role-Taking Skill

Catherine R. Cooper
Harold D. Grotevant
Sherri M. Condon

Although the adolescent's competence is typically judged in terms of the success with which the adolescent has been launched into worlds outside the family, little is known about individual differences in such competence, and few studies have attempted to account for them. This chapter focuses on the family as a context for the development of two aspects of psychosocial competence in late adolescence: a sense of identity and role-taking skill.

This work was supported by grants from the National Institute of Child Health and Human Development and the Hogg Foundation for Mental Health and from the University Research Institute and the Institute of Human Development and Family Studies of the University of Texas at Austin. We express our appreciation to the 121 families who generously shared their time by participating in the project. We especially thank Susan Ayers-Lopez, Tim Gregg, Patricia Griffin Heilbrun, Thomas Hoeffner, Linda Lamb, Margaret Meyer, and Laura Seymer, staff members who contributed to the completion of the project with extraordinary dedication, intelligence, and fine colleagueship, and Linde Soderquist for her assistance with the preparation of the manuscript.

H. D. Grotevant and C. R. Cooper (Eds.). *Adolescent Development in the Family.* New Directions for Child Development, no. 22. San Francisco: Jossey-Bass, December 1983.

43

Our general approach to the study of families is transactional. It recognizes that the directions of influence in the family include multiple and reciprocal pathways. It is consistent with theoretical statements by Belsky (1981), Hartup (1979, 1983), Lerner (Lerner and Spanier, 1978), Sameroff (1975), and Lewis (Lewis and Feiring, 1979), who all have emphasized the importance of understanding the development of the child within the context of family relationships. However, we have also incorporated constructs concerning the relation between family process and adolescent development derived from family systems theory into our investigation. Family systems theory (for example, Beavers, 1977; Broderick and Smith, 1979; Hill, 1971; Lewis and others, 1976) is seen as especially appropriate for this work for three reasons. First, it acknowledges the multidirectionality of influences within the family. Second, it facilitates the conceptualization of each person in the family as a developing individual and of the whole family as a changing mix of competencies and needs (R. Hill, 1979). Third, it permits us to conceptualize subsystems within the family, relations among these subsystems, and roles that individuals play within various family subsystems.

The vast majority of the empirical work concerning the launching of the child into worlds outside the family has focused on infants and preschool children. Several studies have demonstrated, for example, that the security of the mother-child attachment is predictive of the child's later effectiveness in peer relations (Lieberman, 1977; Waters and others, 1979) and in independent exploration of spatial environments (Hazen and Durrett, 1982). This theme has been extended by Hartup (1979) and Hill (1980), who have proposed that security in family relationships can promote competence by allowing the adolescent to become engaged with worlds outside the family, including the domain of peer relationships as well as experiences that facilitate the achievement of identity.

The literature on adolescent development within the family tends to emphasize the primacy of either autonomy or connectedness in family interaction. Psychoanalytic conceptualizations in particular have portrayed adolescence as a time of storm and stress, during which autonomy can be achieved only by breaking away from the parents and severing infantile object ties (Blos, 1979; Coleman, 1978). The opposite view, that adolescence is a placid time marked in most families by little parent-adolescent conflict and by strong agreement on basic values, has been taken by some researchers working with nonclinical populations (Offer, 1969; Offer and others, 1981).

Our research (Cooper and others, 1983; Grotevant and Cooper, 1982) indicates that both individuality and connectedness in family relationships are important in adolescent development. Consistent with our views are those of systems-oriented family therapists, who have stressed the importance of the balance between individuality and connectedness in the family as a predictor both of family health and of children's individual competence (Minuchin, 1974; Olson and others, 1979).

This chapter has two purposes: first, to present the model of family
communication that we developed in order to examine links between family
system functioning and adolescent development; second, to report a test of the
proposition that family processes indicative of individuality and connectedness
can predict the adolescent's effectiveness in identity exploration and role-
taking skill. In this chapter, we will focus primarily on measures of the parent-
child relationship as one approach to the larger issue of conceptualizing whole-
family system dynamics. For analyses of the role of the marital relationship in
adolescent development, see Cooper and others (1983).

Individuation: A Model of Process in Family Systems

In earlier stages of our research, we drew on insights from family systems theory and family therapy to identify aspects of family communication
that seem to enhance adolescent psychosocial competence. Specifically, we
considered the work of clinicians who emphasized the importance of both individuality and connectedness in developing a sense of identity, in having a distinctive point of view, and in being able to coordinate multiple points of view
(Lewis and others, 1976; Minuchin, 1974; Riskin and Faunce, 1972; Walsh,
1982). We used this work to develop a model of individuation. We view individuation as a relationship property (Huston and Robins, 1982), not as a characteristic of individuals or whole families, because one can have individuated
relationships with some people and not with others. However, one particular
individual may be more likely than others to establish individuated relationships. Individuation is not seen as a property of whole families because the
quality of relationships within a family can vary across dyads and over time.
However, some particular families may have uniformly individuated or nonindividuated relationships.

As a description of a relationship, individuation is consistent with conceptualizations of systems-oriented clinicians, such as Minuchin (1974) and
Olson (Olson and others, 1979), who view family cohesion as a dimension
with two extremes: enmeshment—a high degree of connectedness, in which
family members are expected to act and think alike—and disengagement—a
low degree of connectedness, in which family members are highly independent
and have little effect on one another. For our purposes, we defined the individuated relationship as one that displays a balance between individuality and
connectedness.

Our model of individuation served as a framework for the identification of a set of communication patterns indicative of individuality and connectedness in relationships. In earlier work we examined the factorial compo-
sition of these behavioral indicators of individuality by means of factor analysis (Grotevant and Cooper, 1982). Four distinct factors emerged: Two factors
reflect aspects of individuality, and two reflect aspects of connectedness. The
aspects of individuality include self-assertion—one's ability to have a point of

view and to communicate it clearly — and separateness — one's ability to express the differentness of self from others. Connectedness is indicated by permeability — the expression of openness or responsiveness to the views of others — and mutuality — the expression of sensitivity to or respect for the ideas of others. These four factors and the communication behaviors indicative of each are presented in Table 1.

Two Key Adolescent Developmental Tasks: Identity Formation and Role Taking

Identity Formation. As a consequence both of their physical and cognitive development and of changing social expectations, adolescents begin to reevaluate and reorganize the skills and identifications of childhood into a new - framework that provides the adolescent with a "subjective sense of invigorating sameness and continuity" (Erikson, 1968, p. 19). Identity formation necessitates the use of social cognitive and social comparison processes. These processes require one to look critically at oneself and at society simultaneously — in other words, to engage in multiple perspective taking (J. P. Hill, 1979). Identity is also dynamic; new elements are added from time to time (Marcia, 1980). As this gradual process of change takes place, the entire gestalt of one's identity can change. The distinctive and important feature of identity in adolescence is that adolescence provides the first opportunity for a sense of self to be based on mature cognitive and social cognitive abilities.

In societies that provide their members with a variety of life choices, identity formation is approached in several different content areas, including occupational choice, political beliefs, religious and philosophical beliefs, sex roles, interpersonal relationships, and sexual identity. The process of identity formation in each area involves two aspects: exploration — active consideration of alternative possibilities — and commitment — certainty of a decision. In this chapter, we will focus on the relation between the dynamics of the adolescent's family and the adolescent's freedom and ability to explore possibilities for the future.

Role Taking. Role taking includes the ability to conceive of the distinctive perceptual, cognitive, and affective experiences and perspectives of another person and to consider those perspectives in subsequent thinking and behavior (Rubin and Everett, 1982). Research findings indicate that developmental change in role taking continues well into middle childhood and adolescence (Hill and Palmquist, 1978; Shantz, 1975). For example, advanced role taking has been observed in the context of persuasion tasks, when adolescents anticipate their parents' potential counterarguments or describe the advantages of acquiescence to their requests (Clark and Delia, 1976).

In Selman's (Selman, 1980; Stone and Selman, 1982) structural model of invariant stages in the development of perspective taking, preadolescents

Table 1. Conceptual Dimensions and Behavioral Indexes of Individuation

Self-Assertion: Displays awareness of own point of view and responsibility for communicating it clearly
1. Suggests Action or Location Directly (.63)[a]
   Examples:
   a. Something I've always wanted to do—to go up to the northwest part of the country.
   b. I'd like to go to Italy.

Permeability: Expresses responsiveness to the views of others
1. Acknowledgement (.78)
   a. You said go to Canada.
   b. Oh.
   c. Uh huh.
   d. Okay.
2. Requests Information/Validation (.72)
   a. In what perspective?
   b. What is a rail?
   c. How far is it from Rome to Athens?
3. Agrees with/Incorporates Other's Ideas (.46)
   a. I'd like to go there, too.
   b. Yeah, Yellowstone.
   c. Let's use Jim's idea of Spain and go to Madrid.
4. Relevant Comment (.39)
   a. So, we have two weeks and unlimited funds.
   b. Spain is next to France.
   c. Rail express. (elaborates response)
5. Complies with Request for Action (.28)
   a. I'll write that down right now.
   b. Okay.

Mutuality: Shows sensitivity and respect for other's views
1. Suggests Action or Location Indirectly (.92)
   a. Let's go to Canada.
   b. Would either of you like to go back to Italy?
2. Initiates Compromise (.41)
   a. While Mom's in the antique shop, we can hike for a while.
   b. We can take Cindy to the Bahamas, and then we can go wherever you want to go.
3. States Other's Feelings (.32)
   a. The kids will love to see Disneyworld.
   b. Your mother has always wanted to go to England.
4. Answers Request for Information/Validation (.30)
   a. A rail you go by train.
   b. It's about 400 miles.

Separateness: Expresses distinctiveness of self from others
1. Requests Action (.51)
   a. Write that down there.
   b. Wait a minute.
   c. Let's vote on it.

Table 1. Conceptual Dimensions and Behavioral Indexes of Individuation
(continued)

    2. Disagrees/Challenges Other's Idea Directly (.46)
       a. I don't want to go on a train.
       b. No.
    3. Disagrees/Challenges Other's Idea Indirectly (.29)
       a. But, two or three months.
       b. We don't have time to do all that.
       c. Why do you want to go there?
    4. Irrelevant Comment (.33)
       a. I'd like some more tea.
       b. You know, we're missing my favorite show.

[a] Factor loading of communication behavior on its primary factor.

are beginning to be able to reflect on the nature of their relationships from the point of view of a third person. The final stage is characterized by the ability to coordinate "all possible third perspectives — a societal perspective. At this level, the subject can compare and qualitatively contrast sets and levels of perspectives" (1976, p. 160). Yussen (1976), whose subjects completed a moral reasoning questionnaire from the perspective of the self, a typical policeman, and a typical philosopher, found increases with age across ninth-, tenth-, and twelfth-grade students and college subjects in the ability to differentiate among social roles. Thus, simultaneous coordination of two or more perspectives can be seen to improve through late adolescence.

    Although adolescents typically appreciate the existence of different perspectives and the general need for role taking, they can lack the inferential skills needed to compute and coordinate multiple perspectives, or they can fail to apply these insights in particular circumstances (Feffer and Gourevitch, 1960; Flavell and others, 1968) or relationships, such as their relationship with their parents (Blos, 1979). Then too, culturally distinctive experiences accrued during childhood can channel subsequent role taking into a variety of specializations ranging from altruistic to conning in nature (Turner, 1956).

    In summary, both identity formation and mature role-taking ability require the adolescent to possess a viewpoint, to be aware of others' views, and both to integrate and to differentiate his or her own views from those of others. In identity, these skills can be seen in the identification and active exploration of alternatives for the future and in the integration of these possibilities into a coherent, consistent sense of self. In role taking, these skills can be seen in the identification of other social perspectives and in the coordination of these perspectives into an interpersonally viable mode of relating to others. Wide individual differences exist in adolescents' capacity to employ these skills, because their application is greatly influenced by contextual factors and because individual differences exist in the cognitive skills on which they are based (Hill and Palmquist, 1978). However, unlike some cognitive attainments, neither of these domains of social cognitive development has a clear end point, and neither involves a single criterial achievement. Rather, their domains of application continue to evolve with changes in demands, opportunities, and relationships during the individual's life.

Thus, the goal of our research is to trace empirically the contribution that individuality and connectedness in family communication make to adolescent identity formation and role-taking skill. The model of individuation within the family provides the basis for identifying communication behaviors that we anticipate will predict these adolescent developmental outcomes. By examining interaction patterns in typical families, we hope to develop an account of the processes through which interaction within the family can enhance the adolescent's development in domains beyond the family.

Method

Subjects. The subjects in our study were members of eighty-four Caucasian middle-class two-parent families. Each family included an adolescent who was a high school senior and one or two siblings. The target adolescents included forty-six females and thirty-eight males. The families were drawn from a sample of 121 families who participated in the Family Process Project, which was directed by the two senior authors. In all eighty-four families, four members—two adults and two children—participated in the Family Interaction Task.

Procedures. Each family participated in two data collection sessions. The first, which involved both parents, the target adolescent, and one sibling, took place in the family's home. Measures administered included the Family Interaction Task (to the whole family), the Ego Identity Interview (to the target adolescent), and the Extended Range Vocabulary Test (to each family member). During a later session at the university, the adolescent participated in a number of tasks, including the Role-Taking Task.

Family Interaction Task. The Family Interaction Task (FIT) was designed to elicit active participation from all family members in a task in which the adolescent's interest and expertise could contribute to the family's decisions. The family was asked to make plans together for a two-week vacation, for which they had unlimited funds. Their task was to plan the day-by-day itinerary, listing both the location and the activity planned for each day. The research assistant gave them twenty minutes in which to reach their decision, turned on a tape recorder, and left the room.

The analysis of family communication patterns was based on work in speech and conversational analysis (for example, Dore, 1979; Coulthard, 1977) that concentrates not on the grammatical form of each utterance, but on the interpersonal function and on the way in which participants in conversation collaborate in order to sustain interaction.

Verbatim transcripts of the FIT were made from the audiotapes. Using transcripts and tapes, coders assigned each of the first 300 utterances of the interaction to one of six move categories and to one of eight response categories operationalizing the dimensions of individuation. Cooper and others (1982) discuss this time-sampling strategy. The organization of the code items, which are listed and defined in Table 1, reflects the fact that some utterances appear both to direct or move the conversation and to respond to previous utterances by other participants. Interjudge reliabilities among coders exceeded 75 percent agreement for all categories but Acknowledgements and Initiates Compromise. Each transcript was reviewed by a linguist (Condon), and discrepancies were resolved by consultation with the coding manual (Condon and others, 1981). All FIT coders were blind with respect to the adolescents' performance and to all other measures. The data were submitted to factor analysis, using principal-factor solution with varimax rotation (Nie and others, 1975). This analysis yielded four factors that together accounted for 51.3 percent of the variance. The loadings of the fourteen communication behaviors on their primary factors are presented in Table 1.

Ego Identity Interview. The Ego Identity Interview, developed by Marcia (1966) and revised and extended by Grotevant and Cooper (1981), operationalizes Erikson's (1950, 1968) construct of identity in six areas that are pertinent developmentally for both male and female high school students in the United States (Grotevant and others, 1982): occupational choice, religion, politics, friendships, dating, and sex roles.

Each interview was administered by a trained interviewer of the same sex as the subject, and the interview was tape-recorded; the median length of these interviews was approximately forty-five minutes. Each tape was rated independently by two trained research assistants, who were blind to the hypotheses of the study and to the adolescent's performance on other measures. Disagreements were resolved by a third independent rater. Percent exact agreement between two raters averaged 80.7 percent for interviews of females and 79.6 percent for interviews of males. Percent agreement for two out of three raters averaged 97.3 percent for female subjects and 96.6 percent for male subjects. The identity exploration score was the sum of the exploration ratings across these six domains (possible range: 6–24). Adolescents receiving the highest ratings had actively considered a wide variety of options for themselves (reflecting breadth) by exploring each option in a variety of ways (reflecting depth).

Role-Taking Task. During the second session, each adolescent was administered Feffer's (Feffer, 1959; Feffer and Suchotliff, 1966) Role-Taking Task (RTT), which was designed to assess the degree to which the adolescent could differentiate and coordinate multiple points of view. In the RTT, the adolescent was shown a stimulus picture of three individuals (facing away from the viewer) in a kitchen scene. The individuals were an adult male, an adult female, and an adolescent of the same gender as the subject. The subject was first asked to make up a dramatic story about the actors in the picture, then to retell the story three times, once from the perspective of each person. Transcripts of the audiotaped stories were coded according to Feffer (1959). Lower scores indicate a lack of reciprocal perspective taking between characters, while higher scores indicate increasing coordination of perspectives of a psychological rather than action nature. RTTs were scored independently by four judges, who were unaware of the adolescent's performance on other tasks. Three of the four judges agreed on the exact score at least 80 percent of the time. Disagreements were discussed and resolved by the group.

Vocabulary. The Extended Range Vocabulary Test (Ekstrom and others, 1976) was administered to each family member to determine the association of individual differences in performance on other measures with verbal ability. The test consisted of forty-eight words with five responses each given in two timed, six-minute sessions.

Results and Discussion

The relations between the process variables from the Family Interaction Task and both identity exploration and role taking will be discussed in two parts. First, quantitative findings will be presented for the father, mother, and target adolescent. The presentation will be based on three analyses: simple correlations of the frequencies of FIT communication behaviors with identity exploration ratings and role-taking scores; stepwise multiple regressions of exploration and role taking on sets of father's, mother's, and adolescent's communication behaviors and the factor scores from the four factors of individuation; and *t*-test contrasts between extreme groups of high- and low-scoring adolescents on exploration and role taking for the FIT communication behaviors. Second, qualitative case study material will be used to illustrate the key findings.

Identity Exploration. Several communication patterns of the father were related to the target adolescent's identity exploration rating. Father's expressions of mutuality were positively correlated with exploration both in the correlation and regression analyses. For example, exploration was correlated with father's Initiates Compromise ($r = .21$, $p < .05$) and States Other's Feelings ($r = .19$, $p < .05$). In the regression of exploration on father's communication behaviors, both Initiates Compromise (beta = .27) and States Other's Feelings (beta = .17) were included in the significant regression equation.

Father's expressions of separateness were also related to adolescent exploration. Father's expressions of Disagreements with the mother were positively correlated ($r = .22$, $p < .05$) with adolescent's exploration. When extreme groups of adolescents rating high or low in exploration were compared, we found that the ratio of Disagreements to Permeability expressed by the father to the mother was higher for adolescents with high exploration ratings ($t = 2.41$, $p = .023$), indicating that high identity adolescents were observing disagreements between their parents. In addition, expressions of Permeability from father to mother were higher for the low exploration group ($t = 2.23$, $p = .034$). In contrast, greater Permeability was expressed from the adolescent to the father in the group of high exploring males ($t = 3.89$, $p = .004$).

This pattern suggests that father's supportive communication and reciprocated permeability from the adolescent together create a context conducive to exploration. Perhaps just as the securely attached infant is best able to explore his or her social and physical environment (Ainsworth, 1979), the supported adolescent also senses a secure base from which to explore. However, father's communication patterns do not exclusively involve support. Father's expressions of Disagreements with his wife were also positively correlated with adolescent exploration. Expressions of disagreement from father to mother may create a climate that allows the adolescent to see differences of opinion expressed. This pattern of results points to the need to refine our understanding of the interface between the spouse and parent-adolescent relationships.

A cluster of maternal communication behaviors indicative of Permeability was negatively correlated with adolescent exploration, especially for girls. For example, correlations with exploration were $-.25$ for Requests Information, $-.21$ for Agrees, and $-.20$ for Complies with Requests. These same variables had negative beta weights (-26, $-.17$, and $-.16$ respectively) in the significant regression equation. In addition, low exploring girls had mothers who expressed higher frequencies of Permeability (Requests Information: $t = 2.32$, $p = .038$; Acknowledgements: $t = 2.04$, $p = .059$, and Factor I [Permeability]: $t = 2.44$, $p = .027$).

Mother's behaviors showed positive relationships to adolescent exploration, including Self-Assertion, Initiates Compromise, and States Other's Feelings. Mother's Self-Assertions were positively but modestly related to adolescent exploration: In the regression analysis using communication behaviors, beta was .10; in the regression using factor scores, the beta of Factor IV, Self-Assertion, was .22. Other mother's communication behaviors achieving high betas in the regression equation included Initiates Compromise (.23), Acknowledgments (.18), and States Other's Feelings (.13).

Finally, expression of Disagreement from adolescent to mother was positively correlated with exploration ($r = .24$, $p < .05$). Expression of Permeability from mother to adolescent was negatively correlated with exploration ($r = -.19$, $p < .05$). These results suggest that low exploring adolescent females elicited greater permeability (especially Acknowledgement and Requests for Information) from their mothers. It may be that these mothers were sensing the need of their adolescent daughter for the support and encouragement necessary to become more autonomous or that mothers who behave in oversolicitous ways prevent their daughters from developing autonomy.

Adolescents whose interviews were rated high in identity exploration expressed both separateness and permeability in the FIT. In terms of separateness, exploration was correlated with Indirect Disagreements ($r = .36$, $p < .001$). In addition, both Direct and Indirect Disagreements were significant predictors in the regression equation (beta = .19 and .36, respectively). This pattern was confirmed in the extreme group contrast: Indirect Disagreements were more frequently expressed by high exploring adolescents than by low exploring adolescents ($t = 2.44$, $p = .027$), and Direct Disagreements were more frequently expressed by high exploring females than by low exploring females ($t = 2.16$, $p = .047$). In addition, exploration was positively related to adolescent permeability. The correlation between Acknowledgement and exploration was .27 ($p < .01$), and adolescent Factor I (Permeability) was the best predictor of exploration in the regression of exploration on FIT factor scores (beta = .24).

These findings are consistent with Erikson's (1968) view of the task of identity as the need to define a sense of oneself as distinctive from others. Disagreement is one way of expressing this difference. At the same time, because identity formation requires the consideration, selection, and integration of possible sources of information about the self and about others, permeability facilitates the adolescent's gaining access to this information.

Role-Taking Task. Father's Initiation of Compromise among the ideas of others was positively related to adolescent's role-taking scores in both the correlational analysis ($r = .30$, $p < .01$) and in the significant multiple regression equation (beta = .24). Similarly, when adolescents scoring at the extremes on role taking were compared, the fathers of high-scoring subjects modeled higher frequencies of Initiating Compromise ($t = 2.60$, $p = .013$). However, there was a negative association between father's Complying with Requests and adolescent's role-taking scores ($r = -.27$, $p < .01$). Thus, these adolescents had more opportunities both to observe differences in points of view and to experience their father's integrating multiple perspectives. An intriguing pattern was observed in a group of negative associations between mother's communication behaviors and adolescent's RTT score. Inspection of the communication patterns among the families of the lowest- and highest-scoring girls revealed that mothers of the low-scoring girls were producing greater frequencies of Direct Self-Assertions ($t = 2.23$, $p = .044$), Acknowledgements ($t = 2.24$, $p = .041$), and Requests for Actions ($t = 2.33$, $p = .03$) as well as of most other utterance types, as if they were filling in when their daughter was not contributing. In contrast, the mothers of low-scoring boys were producing higher numbers of Direct Disagreements ($t = 2.74$, $p = .015$). One possible explanation for these patterns is suggested by the positive association between RTT scores and vocabulary ($r = .27$, $p < .01$). That is, low-scoring adolescents may be functioning at a less advanced intellectual level and elicit maternal reactions that differ according to gender: more compensatory protectiveness toward daughters and more abrasiveness toward sons.

Examination of the target adolescents' own communication behaviors suggests the picture of the high role-taking adolescent as an open individual. Adolescents' RTT scores were positively associated with the frequency with which they Requested Information from others ($r = .20$, $p < .05$) and negatively with Directing the Actions of others ($r = -.25$, $p < .05$). It is notable that RTT performance was also associated with identity exploration ($r = .31$, $p < .01$).

Qualitative Findings. The link between family communication patterns and adolescent development can be illustrated by examining two individual families in detail. One family exemplifies individuation in relationships, the other a lack of such individuation. The interactions in Carol's family most closely approximated the relationship property of individuation. Her father's opening statement on the Family Interaction Task set the tone for the interaction: "I think probably what we all ought to do is decide the things that we want to do, each one of us individually. And, then maybe we'll be able to reconcile from that point. . . . Let's go ahead and take a few minutes to decide where we'd like to go and what we would like to do. And, maybe we'll be able to work everything everybody wants to do in these fourteen days. Okay?" All three family members were active and involved; humor, candor, spontaneity, and vulnerability were all displayed. For example, the mother commented, "I think we all have good imaginations," while the father said, "I think that's kind of nice. I think we ought to be a rich gang."

Carol seemed to be aware of her role in the family and of the boundary between the adolescent and parental generations. During her identity interview, she said, "I have a say but not a deciding vote in family decisions." Carol's identity exploration rating of 18 was very high. A distinctive quality of her identity exploration was that she experienced her parents as providing room for her to explore beyond their own experiences or needs. For example, she reported that both parents felt that religion had been forced on them as children, so they decided not to force it on her. Consequently, she had been able to explore several religions as possible alternatives with her friends. In the domain of friendship, Carol had maintained a relationship with a girl who had been a close friend but who later became involved with drugs and turned against her parents. Carol had been able to maintain this relationship and see how it differed from her other close friendships without compromising her own standards. Her parents were concerned about this friendship, but they trusted Carol and permitted her to work through this situation. In a comparable pattern, Carol's score of 15 on the Role-Taking Task was also very high. She achieved the highest reciprocal level score by clearly coordinating the perspective of two characters in her story and by elaborating both their external and psychological states.

In contrast, the family of Janet, the firstborn of two, reflected nonindividuated spousal and parent-child relationships with few disagreements, self-assertions that largely coincided with the family's point of view, and frequent expressions of connectedness. The ratio of agreements to disagreements between mother and father (16) was unusually high, suggesting a marked imbalance between expression of individuality and connectedness. In addition, Janet disagreed with her father only once, and he never disagreed with her, whereas she was responsive to him twenty-nine times, and he was responsive to her ten times. Enmeshment in this family's interaction was illustrated in the first five utterances on the Family Interaction Task:

Mother: Where shall we go?
Father: Back to Spain.
Mother: Back to Spain.
Janet: Back to Spain.
Sister: Back to Spain.

When Janet's father later asked for more suggestions, she said, "And then, I don't. . . I mean, you go on, Dad, 'cause I don't know. . . what else."

Janet's low identity exploration rating of 13 may reflect a lack of exploration of issues outside the consensual family beliefs. In this family, in which signs of individuated spousal and parent-child relationships were less evident, the necessity for agreement and connectedness among family members and the family members' excessive involvement in each other's identity appeared to hinder the adolescent's development of individual ideas regarding career, dating, and other issues. With regard to career choice, Janet commented, "I'm having a hard time deciding what to do. It would be easier if they would tell me what to do, but of course I don't want that."

Janet's low role-taking score of 9 suggests a lack of ability to express both separate and reciprocal points of view. While telling her story, Janet commented, "I don't know what the others are thinking, because I'm thinking of it only as if I'm the girl." Perhaps the nonindividuated communication patterns that Janet observed in her parents' relationship and that she participated in with her father inhibited her ability both to engage in identity exploration and to coordinate different perspectives.

Conclusions

This chapter has reported the first findings from an investigation of the relation between patterns of communication in family systems and adolescent psychosocial development. The phase reported here has yielded evidence that both individuality and connectedness in family interaction are adaptive for adolescent development. Our model of individuation, with its four factors, has provided a differentiated approach to understanding both individuality and connectedness as they occur in the family system. Self-assertion—the expression of one's own point of view—and separateness—the expression of differences in views between self and others—can be seen as different modes of expressing a distinct or separate perspective within the family. In contrast, permeability—expressing responsiveness and openness to other's ideas—and mutuality—showing sensitivity or respect in relating to others—involve different aspects of support or connectedness within the family. Further, the

56

operationalization of these factors illustrates that neither individuality nor connectedness is unidimensional. For example, father's Initiation of Compromise, a measure of mutuality, showed positive relationships with both adolescent identity exploration and role taking, whereas frequency of Agreements, a measure of permeability, did not.

Our understanding of these four dimensions and the processes that they reflect will be enhanced as we pursue the next questions of our research. Our next steps are directed to a different level of analysis, that of the relationship. We are tracing the contribution that the co-occurrence of the qualities of individuality and connectedness within particular relationships in the family makes to adolescent identity formation and role-taking skill. We anticipate that families in which the adolescent oberves or participates in an individuated relationship are more likely to foster these qualities.

In conclusion, it seems appropriate to reconsider the developmental needs of the adolescent who is about to leave home. Our findings suggest that the leaving process is facilitated by individuated family relationships, characterized by separateness, which gives the adolescent permission to develop his or her own point of view, in the context of connectedness, which provides a secure base from which the adolescent can explore worlds outside the family.

References

Ainsworth, M. D. S. "Infant-Mother Attachment." *American Psychologist,* 1979, *34,* 932–937.
Beavers, W. R. *Psychotherapy and Growth: A Family Systems Perspective.* New York: Brunner/Mazel, 1977.
Belsky, J. "Early Human Experience: A Family Perspective." *Developmental Psychology,* 1981, *17,* 3–23.
Blos, P. "The Second Individuation Process." In P. Blos (Ed.), *The Adolescent Passage.* New York: International University Press, 1979.
Broderick, C. J., and Smith, J. "The General Systems Approach to the Family." In W. R. Burr, R. Hill, F. I. Nye, and I. Reiss (Eds.), *Contemporary Theories about the Family.* Vol. 2. New York: Free Press, 1979.
Clark, R. A., and Delia, J. G. "The Development of Functional Persuasive Skills in Childhood and Early Adolescence." *Child Development,* 1976, *47,* 1008–1014.
Coleman, J. C. "Current Contradictions in Adolescent Theory." *Journal of Youth and Adolescence,* 1978, *7,* 1–11.
Condon, S. M., Cooper, C. R., and Grotevant, H. D. *Manual for the Analysis of Family Discourse.* Austin: University of Texas, 1981.
Cooper C. R., Grotevant, H. D., and Condon, S. M. "Methodological Challenges of Selectivity in Family Interaction: Addressing Temporal Patterns of Individuation." *Journal of Marriage and the Family,* 1982, *44,* 749–754.
Cooper, C. R., Grotevant, H. D., Moore, M. S., and Condon, S. M. "Predicting Adolescent Role Taking and Identity Exploration from Family Communication Patterns: A Comparison of One- and Two-Child Families." In T. Falbo (Ed.), *The Single-Child Family.* New York: Guilford Press, 1983.
Coulthard, M. *An Introduction to Discourse Analysis.* Essex, England: Longman House, 1977.

Dore, J. "Conversational Acts and the Acquisition of Language." In E. Ochs and B. B. Schieffelin (Eds.), *Developmental Pragmatics.* New York: Academic Press, 1979.

Ekstrom, R. B., French, J. W., Harman, H. H., and Derman, D. *Manual for Kit of Factor-Referenced Cognitive Tests.* Princeton, N.J.: Educational Testing Service, 1976.

Erikson, E. H. *Childhood and Society.* New York: Norton, 1950.

Erikson, E. H. *Identity: Youth and Crisis.* New York: Norton, 1968.

Feffer, M. H. "The Cognitive Implications of Role Taking Behavior." *Journal of Personality,* 1959, *27,* 152–168.

Feffer, M. H., and Gourevitch, S. "Cognitive Aspects of Role Taking in Children." *Journal of Personality,* 1960, *28,* 383–396.

Feffer, M. H., and Suchotliff, L. "Decentering Implications of Social Interaction." *Journal of Personality and Social Psychology,* 1966, *4,* 415–422.

Flavell, J., Botkin, P. T., Fry, C. L., Wright, J. W., and Jarvis, R. W. *The Development of Role-Taking Skills in Children.* New York: Wiley, 1968.

Grotevant, H. D., and Cooper, C. R. "Assessing Adolescent Identity in the Areas of Occupation, Religion, Politics, Friendship, Dating, and Sex Roles: Manual for Administration and Coding of the Interview." *JSAS Catalog of Selected Documents in Psychology,* 1981, *11,* 52 (Ms. No. 2295).

Grotevant, H. D., and Cooper, C. R. *Identity Formation and Role-Taking Skill in Adolescence: An Investigation of Family Structure and Family Process Antecedents.* Final report prepared for the National Institute of Child Health and Human Development, University of Texas at Austin, 1982.

Grotevant, H. D., Thorbecke, W. L., and Meyer, M. L. "An Extension of Marcia's Identity Status Interview into the Interpersonal Domain." *Journal of Youth and Adolescence,* 1982, *11,* 33–47.

Hartup, W. W. "The Social Worlds of Childhood." *American Psychologist,* 1979, *34,* 944–950.

Hartup, W. W. "The Peer System." In P. H. Mussen and E. M. Hetherington (Eds.), *Carmichael's Manual of Child Psychology.* (4th ed.) New York: Wiley, 1983.

Hazen, N. L., and Durrett, M. E. "Relationship of Security of Attachment to Exploration and Cognitive Mapping Abilities in Two-Year-Olds." *Developmental Psychology,* 1982, *18,* 751–759.

Hill, J. P. Personal communication, August 1979.

Hill, J. P. "The Early Adolescent and the Family." In *The Seventy-Ninth Yearbook of the National Society for the Study of Education,* 1980.

Hill, J. P., and Palmquist, W. J. "Social Cognition and Social Relations in Early Adolescence." *International Journal of Behavioral Development,* 1978, *1,* 1–36.

Hill, R. "Modern Systems Theory and the Family: A Confrontation." *Social Science Information,* 1971, *10,* (5), 7–26.

Hill, R. "The Future of Child and Family Research." Panel discussion presented at the International Seminar on the Child and Family, St. Peter, Minn., August 1979.

Huston, T. L., and Robins, E. "Conceptual and Methodological Issues in Studying Close Relationships." *Journal of Marriage and the Family,* 1982, *44,* 901–925.

Lerner, R. M., and Spanier, G. B. (Eds.). *Child Influences on Marital and Family Interaction: A Life Span Perspective.* New York: Academic Press, 1978.

Lewis, J. M., Beavers, W. R., Gossett, J. T., and Phillips, V. A. *No Single Thread: Psychological Health in Family Systems.* New York: Brunner/Mazel, 1976.

Lewis, J., and Feiring, C. "The Child's Social Network: Social Object, Social Functions, and Their Relationship." In M. Lewis and L. A. Rosenblum (Eds.), *The Child and Its Family.* New York: Plenum, 1979.

Lieberman, A. F. "Preschoolers' Competence with a Peer: Relations with Attachment and Peer Experience." *Child Development,* 1977, *48,* 1277–1287.

58

Marcia, J. E. "Development and Validation of Ego Identity Status." *Journal of Personality and Social Psychology,* 1966, *3,* 551–558.

Marcia, J. E. "Identity in Adolescence." In J. Adelson (Ed.), *Handbook of Adolescent Psychology.* New York: Wiley, 1980.

Minuchin, S. *Families and Family Therapy.* Cambridge, Mass.: Harvard University Press, 1974.

Nie, N. H., Hull, C. H., Jenkins, J. G., Steinbrenner, K., and Bent, D. H. *Statistical Packages for the Social Sciences.* (2nd ed.) New York: McGraw-Hill, 1975.

Offer, D. *The Psychological World of the Teenager.* New York: Basic Books, 1969.

Offer, D., Ostrov, E., and Howard, K. I. *The Adolescent: A Psychological Self-Portrait.* New York: Basic Books, 1981.

Olson, D. H., Sprenkle, D. H., and Russell, C. S. "Circumplex Model of Marital and Family Systems, I: Cohesion and Adaptability Dimensions, Family Types, and Clinical Applications." *Family Process,* 1979, *18,* 3–28.

Riskin, J., and Faunce, E. E. "An Evaluative Review of Family Interaction Research." *Family Process,* 1972, *11,* 365–455.

Rubin, K. H., and Everett, B. "Social Perspective Taking in Young Children." In S. G. Moore and C. R. Cooper (Eds.), *The Young Child: Reviews of Research.* Vol. 3. Washington, D.C.: National Association for the Education of Young Children, 1982.

Sameroff, A. J. "Early Influences on Development: Fact or Fancy?" *Merrill-Palmer Quarterly,* 1975, *21,* 267–294.

Selman, R. L. "Toward a Structural Analysis of Developing Interpersonal Relations Concepts: Research with Normal and Disturbed Preadolescent Boys." In A. D. Pick (Ed.), *Minnesota Symposia on Child Psychology,* Minneapolis: University of Minnesota Press, 1976.

Selman, R. L. *The Growth of Interpersonal Understanding: Developmental and Clinical Analyses.* New York: Academic Press, 1980.

Shantz, C. U. "The Development of Social Cognition." In E. M. Hetherington (Ed.), *Review of Child Development Research.* Vol. 5. Chicago: University of Chicago Press, 1975.

Stone, C. R., and Selman, R. L. "A Structural Approach to Research in the Development of Interpersonal Behavior Among Grade School Children." In K. H. Rubin and H. S. Ross (Eds.), *Peer Relationships and Social Skills in Childhood.* New York: Springer-Verlag, 1982.

Turner, R. H. "Role-Taking, Role Standpoint, and Reference Group Behavior." *American Journal of Sociology,* 1956, *61,* 316–328.

Turner, R. *Family Interaction.* New York: Wiley, 1970.

Walsh, F. (Ed.). *Normal Family Processes.* New York: Guilford Press, 1982.

Waters, E., Wippman, J., and Sroufe, L. A. "Attachment, Positive Affect, and Competence in the Peer Group: Two Studies in Construct Validation." *Child Development,* 1979, *50,* 821–829.

Yussen, S. R. "Moral Reasoning from the Perspective of Others." *Child Development,* 1976, *47,* 551–555.

Catherine R. Cooper is associate professor in the Department of Home Economics, Division of Child Development and Family Relationships, and in the Department of Psychology at the University of Texas at Austin. Her research interests concern the role of communication in the development of relationships, both within the family and in peer groups.

Harold D. Grotevant is associate professor in the Department of Home Economics, Division of Child Development and Family Relationships, and in the Department of Psychology at the University of Texas at Austin. He is especially interested in the contribution of the family to adolescent identity formation and career development.

Sherri M. Condon completed her Ph.D. in the Department of Linguistics at the University of Texas at Austin and is now professor of Linguistics at Université King Mohamed Hassan II in Rabat, Morocco.

Measures of ego development and psychosocial identity are predictive of differences in the quality of relationships between young adults and their parents.

Young Adults and Their Parents: Individuation to Mutuality

Kathleen M. White
Joseph C. Speisman
Daryl Costos

Late in 1978, with the support of a three-year grant from the National Institute of Mental Health, we began a short-term longitudinal investigation of young adults and their relationships. At the basis of this research was the assumption that not only do individuals have the potential to progress through qualitative developmental changes across the life span but also the relationships in which they participate. In this chapter, we report our first-year findings on the relationships between family relationships and selected aspects of individual functioning.

Why is a study of young adults included in a volume on adolescent development? As we will show, there are some important continuities in the issues in which adolescents and young adults are involved. For example, it seems clear that interrelationships among family interaction patterns, individuation, and other developmental processes continue beyond the adolescent

The study reported in this chapter was supported by a grant from the National Institute of Mental Health (MH31719). Our thanks go to John Houlihan and Catherine Imbasciati for assistance with data analysis and project development and to Daniel Ozer for his comments on an earlier draft.

H. D. Grotevant and C. R. Cooper (Eds.). *Adolescent Development in the Family.* New
Directions for Child Development, no. 22. San Francisco: Jossey-Bass, December 1983.

61

years. Indeed, Klein and others (1978) have argued that the development of each individual family member contributes to the development of various relational networks in the family and that the development of those relational networks contributes to the development of each family member. Moreover, this interplay between individual development and family relationships may be a life span process.

A number of investigators have identified the young adult years as important for the continued evolution of relationships with parents. Studying three generations of family members (the youngest aged sixteen to twenty-six), Bengston and Black (1973) found that perceived solidarity with parents seemed to increase as young adults moved into social positions reflecting adult status. When full adult status was achieved, the level of solidarity expressed by young adults toward their parents was similar to the level of solidarity expressed by those parents toward their own parents.

Bengston and Black's optimistic view of increasing solidarity between young adults and their parents is in sharp contradiction with the findings of a number of other studies, which suggest that the stresses of close relationships can continue to have a negative impact on the interactions between adult children and their parents long after the younger generation emerges from adolescence. For example, Cox (1970) found that thirty-year-olds found it difficult to comprehend the viewpoint of their elders and to express compassionate acceptance when they disagreed. Cox noted that even at age thirty her subjects expressed disenchantment with their elders with rigorous frankness. Indeed, she says (1970, p. 221), "a state of uneasy truce is characteristic of the relationship with parents of more than half of these young people, while a sixth of them are angry and condemning. Only a third of the group genuinely enjoy and value their parents."

Concerned that no significant progress had been made in the conceptualization of developmental stages after the identity struggle of youth, Gould (1972) undertook several studies of changes in object relations (that is, in intimate attachment relationships) during the adult years. On the basis of his observations, Gould (1972, p. 525) concluded that, while individuals aged sixteen to twenty-two are concerned with getting away from their parents, young people in the twenty-two- to twenty-eight-year age group "see their parents as people with whom they want to establish a *modus vivendi* but to whom they still have to prove their competence as adults."

It is likely that apparent inconsistencies among these and other relevant studies stem partly from sampling issues and partly from the differing orientations of the investigators — for example, toward identifying general developmental patterns or toward examining individual and group differences in development. Keniston's work on youth in the 1960s, especially on radical youth, is relevant to both issues. Commenting on interviews with young radicals involved in the Vietnam protest of summer 1967, Keniston (1968, p. 67) postulated that "many young men and women still find it impossible to present a differentiated portrait of their parents, and much questioning is required before any picture of their parents as people begins to emerge. With these young radicals, however, the ability to differentiate between the parents and between different aspects of each parent's character and behavior was highly developed. They seemed unusually able to tolerate ambivalence, to explain parental behavior with its probable causes, to combine praise and affection with the recognition of defects. Their life histories indicate this capacity was not achieved without struggle."

What is the basis for individual and group differences in the evolution of relationships with parents? What kinds of experiences or abilities help young adults with the developmental task, described by Levinson (1978), of rejecting certain aspects of their earlier relationships, sustaining other aspects, and building in new qualities, such as mutual respect between distinctive individuals? And, what kinds of factors contribute to the achievement of the mature perspective described by Keniston (1968, p. 68) wherein young people can see themselves and their parents as "multidimensional persons, to view them with compassion and understanding, to feel less threatened by their fate and failings, and to be able, if [they choose], to move beyond them"?

There seems to be considerable agreement that young people find it difficult to establish mature, tolerant, mutual relationships with their parents until the young people achieve a certain degree of individuation. (We view individuation more from the perspective of individual psychological development than from the systems perspective adopted by Cooper, Grotevant, and Condon in Chapter Three. Our use of individuation focuses more on issues of autonomy.) Newman and Newman (1975, p. 222) summarize this individuation well: "Once the young person has demonstrated to himself that he can be autonomous, he is able to reestablish a meaningful and more mutual relationship with his family." There also seems to be agreement that such a relationship generally will not emerge during the adolescence of the young person, even during the period that Keniston calls *youth* (approximately eighteen to twenty-two). Again, Newman and Newman (1975) argue that young people are more likely to be alienated from their parents during late adolescence, when the need for autonomy supercedes both dependence and identification, than they are at any other developmental stage.

If these authors are correct, the achievement of autonomy or individuation should facilitate more mutual (and what we would call more mature) relationships with parents. Yet, it also seems likely that many adults become autonomous and well individuated without ever achieving psychological closeness with their parents. At best, individuation may be necessary but not sufficient for the development of mature and mutual relationships between parents and their adult children. What other processes may be involved?

Keniston (1971) links changes in relationships to the individual's levels of ethical and cognitive development. He also notes (1971, p. 16) that developmental transformations are never linked in perfect synchrony: "One young woman may be at a truly adolescent level in her relationships with her parents but at a much later level in moral development." Hinde (1976, p. 13) gives the following example of the kinds of complex mutual influences that may exist between the developmental characteristics of individuals and the nature of their interactions with each other: "[Many] of the qualities of the interactions in a relationship, the kinds of complementariness that can occur, and the ability of the relationship to withstand vicissitudes may be related to the aboslute and relative cognitive levels of the participants. Furthermore, relationships may have special properties depending on the interrelations between the absolute and relative moral and cognitive levels of the participants and other characteristics of the relationship. Thus, relationships involving dominance-submission and nurturance-dependence interactions will differ markedly in character if the partners function at different moral or cognitive levels than if they are similar in these respects."

In our longitudinal project, we are examining the contribution of several dimensions of individual psychological development—for example, ego development, psychosocial development, ethical development—to our own measure of the psychological stage of the relationship with parents. Using retrospective reports on parental childrearing practices, we also have some basis for considering possible precursors of current levels of individual and family functioning. Moreover, we have short-term longitudinal data on other intimate relationships—with girlfriend, boyfriend, or spouse and with children. The report of findings in this chapter is guided by our interest in two major and interrelated processes, individuation and mutuality or connectedness. We see the tension between being separate and being together, between individuation and connectedness, between agency and communion as a lifetime tension, where first one pole, then the other can predominate.

For the purposes of this study, we view individuation in a way that is consistent with the perspective offered by Karpel (1976). According to Karpel, individuation is the process by which a person becomes increasingly differentiated from a past or present relational context. This process, Karpel holds (1976, p. 67), encompasses a multitude of intrapsychic and interpersonal changes that share a common direction: "Individuation involves the subtle but crucial phenomenological shifts by which a person comes to see him/herself as separate and distinct within the relational context in which s/he is embedded." Karpel uses the term *dialogue* to refer to the mature relationships of individuated partners, a notion quite similar to the concept of the individuated family system expressed in Chapter Three.

What does it take for individuated partners to participate in the kind of dialogic relationship that Karpel describes? We believe that, in addition to individuation, both perspective taking—the ability to see issues from the other's point of view—and mutuality—the "democratic" and balanced interactions of peers as opposed to the hierarchical interactions of unequal partners—

are necessary. Individuation, perspective, and mutuality are successive steps in the achievement of fully mature relationships between adults and their parents as assessed by our Family Relationships Interview scoring system. A conceptual underpinning for the relationships among individuation, perspective, and mutuality can be found in cognitive development theory (for example, Loevinger, 1976) and psychosocial developmental theory (for example, Erikson, 1959). Since Loevinger's measure of ego development and Speisman's (Speisman and others, 1983) operationalization of Erikson's psychosocial stages were used in the present study, a brief description of relevant concepts follows.

From Loevinger's (1976, pp. 58–59) perspective, "The essence of the ego is the striving to make sense of experience. The ego is, above all, a process, not a thing." Loevinger has proposed a series of invariant stages of ego development that integrate various frames of reference, including congitive style, interpersonal style, conscious preoccupations, and impulse control. The lower stages of ego development are characterized by impulsive, exploitative, and dependent orientations; the middle levels are typified by conformist thinking; and the higher stages are distinguished by cognitive complexity, autonomy, and respect for individual differences—achievements that, from our perspective, reflect individuation, perspective taking, and the capacity for mutuality. (The conceptual overlap between specific ego and family development stages will be addressed in the methods section of this chapter.)

Erikson (1959) also specifies perspective taking, individuation, and mutual regulation as cornerstones of the life span developmental process, wherein the individual is shaped by the particulars of his or her culture. While Erikson does not provide a measurement process that parallels the procedure of the Family Relationships Interview or of Loevinger's sentence completion test, the conceptual correspondence among these approaches is clear. Erikson's (1959, p. 155) comment on the three adult stages of development illustrates the relevance of his formulation to our own: "The older generation thus needs the younger one as much as the younger one depends on the older, and it would seem that it is in this mutuality of the development of the older and younger generations that certain basic and universal values... become and remain important joint achievements of individual ego development and of the social process."

In undertaking an analysis of the relationships among ego, psychosocial, and family relationships development, we believed that it was crucial to consider the possibility of sex differences. There is considerable evidence that males and females differ in their identity development in important ways (for example, Douvan and Adelson, 1966; see reviews of relevant literature in Matteson, 1975, and Marcia, 1980). Moreover, while the data are inconsistent, some data indicate sex differences in ego development (Block, 1973). Finally, there is evidence for differences between males and females in their expectations of and behavior in close relationships (for example, Levinger and

Raush, 1977). Because of the strong likelihood that patterns of relationship between individual and developmental variables differ for the sexes, all our analyses were done separately by sex.

While our interest was in the relationship among psychological variables, it seemed important not to exclude the role of social status variables from the relationships under consideration. As already mentioned, Bengston and Black (1973) saw entrance into adult social positions (for example, marriage and parenthood) as contributing directly to increased solidarity between children and their parents. Newman and Newman (1975) agree that getting married changes one's relationships with mother and father. Ryder and others (1971) report that having a baby can bring a wife closer to her own mother. Whether the impact of changes in social status relationship with parents varies as a function of sex is very much an open question. Certainly, there is considerable evidence of differences between men and women in their relationships with parents (for example, Hill and others, 1970; Sussman, 1978).

Method

The major question explored in this study was this: Can the developmental stage of an individual's relationship with his or her parents be predicted from scores on measures of ego and psychosocial development? As already noted, data analyses relevant to this question were computed separately by sex, with the contribution of marital status to the outcome variable (family relationship stage) as an important initial step. We do not use the term *family relationship stage* to refer to eras defined by role responsibilities and age of children as family sociologists do. Instead, we define family relationship stage psychologically by reference to such achievements as individuation, perspective, and mature forms of mutuality.

Subjects. From a sample of more than 360 subjects who participated in our combined cross-sectional longitudinal investigation of young adult development and relationships, we selected a subsample of 156 subjects for analysis. This subsample was chosen so as to have ten subjects in each cell when broken down by age, sex, and marital status. We dropped the subsample of twenty-two-year-old married men and women with children because this group was consistently less well educated and more economically disadvantaged than other subject groups. Moreover, we were able to recruit only six twenty-four-year-old married men with children. Out of the 156 subjects, 149 (95.5 percent) were living in separate dwellings from their parents.

Although all subjects were white and the sample was largely middle-class, we achieved some breadth in a number of demographic areas. Nineteen subjects (12.2 percent) had completed their education with a high school or technical school diploma, while forty-five subjects (28.8 percent) had completed some graduate work. A majority of subjects (102, or 65.4 percent) had completed college with a B.A. or B.S. degree, with or without some graduate education.

Of the 136 subjects whose work status was known, two subjects (1.5 percent) were classified as major professionals. Sixty-five (47.8 percent) were lesser professionals, managers, administrators, or proprietors of small businesses. Twenty-three subjects (16.9 percent) were clerical workers, sales personnel, or technicians. Almost twenty percent of our subjects were involved in skilled, semiskilled, or unskilled labor; twenty subjects were unemployed. Finally, fifteen of our female subjects defined themselves as homemakers.

Most subjects came from intact homes. One hundred and twenty-one sets of parents (77.6 percent) were still married and living together. Fifteen subjects (9.6 percent) had parents who were divorced or separated. Twenty-one subjects (13.5 percent) had lost one parent. Finally, most parents had provided their children with some sort of religious upbringing. Sixty-eight subjects (43.6 percent) had been reared in Catholic homes, forty-one (26.3 percent) had been reared in Jewish homes, thirty-seven (23.7 percent) had been reared in Protestant homes, and ten (6.4 percent) had been reared in homes that practiced some other religion or that were agnostic or atheistic.

Measures. Each subject participated in approximately two and one half hours of interviews, including White's Family Relationships Interview, Marcia's Ego Identity Status Interview, Orlofsky's Intimacy Interview, and Selman's Perspective-Taking Interview. Subjects also completed approximately two and one half hours of questionnaire measures intended to tap the same basic areas as the interviews — that is, individual development, family relationships, and dyadic interactions. The relationships between the Family Relationships Interview and a number of the questionnaire measures will be discussed here.

The Family Relationships Interview. Developed specifically for the purpose of this investigation, the Family Relationships Interview (FRI) is a semistructured interview covering four areas: current interactions, resolution of differences of opinion, advice giving, and caretaking. In each area, subjects were asked open-ended questions about their current relationships with their parents, changes in these relationships over time, their view of their parents, their parents' view of them, and the specific behaviors that characterized the interaction.

Each area of the interview is scored separately for the developmental stage of the relationship with the mother and for the developmental stage of the relationship with the father. The stage scoring system ranges from pervasive preoccupation with individuation at stage 1 to a totally mutual peer-like relationship at stage 6. With the inclusion of transitional stages, the stage scoring system converts to a scale scoring system with a potential range of 1 to 11. The defining characteristics of each stage are summarized in Table 1.

What is unique about our scoring system is that what is being scored is not a developmental characteristic of an individual but a developmental characteristic of a relationship as perceived by one party to that relationship. Three major conceptual components underlie the scoring of the relationship: young adult and parent individuation, young adult and parent perspective or role taking, and young adult and parent mutuality. Thus far, only the current

Table 1. Family Relationships Interview Scoring Stages

1 *Individuation.* Subject emphasizes separateness of self from parents. Subject often sees self as right and parents as wrong, self as "up-to-date" and parents as old-fashioned. Subject makes many *I* statements and places much emphasis on fact that he or she is now "grown up."

1/2 Subject is in transition to stage 2, where the emphasis is on the relationship of the parents to the subject and where subject has some perspective on his or her own contribution to the parent-child relationship. Subject begins to acknowledge the importance of the relationship and the subject's participation in a relationship with the parents.

2 *Individuation Plus Perspective on Relationship.* Subject has some perspective on his or her own contribution to the parent-child relationship; for example, by seeing own past role in keeping things stirred up or causing worry. However, what seems like perspective on parents is only perspective on the parents in relation to the self, not perspective on the parents as separate autonomous adults.

2/3 Subject gives evidence of individuation plus signs that he or she is beginning to have some (although not a very fully articulated) perspective on parents and their points of view.

3 *Individuation Plus Perspective on Parents.* Subject gives evidence of individuation plus ability to put self in shoes of parents, see things through their eyes.

3/4 Not only can subject see parents' points of view, but there is evidence that subject has some idea (not very well articulated) of parents' perspectives on subject as individual. Subject gives some evidence that parent sees subject as separate individual.

4 *Individuation Plus Reciprocal Perspectives.* Individuated subject has well-developed perspective on parents plus clear picture of how parents view her or him as an individual. Parents can understand subject as being advice giver, caregiver, having opinions of own. Nevertheless, there is little evidence that subject and parents behave like peers toward each other.

4/5 There is some evidence that in at least a few safe areas subject and parents behave like peers.

5 *Incipient or Pragmatic Mutuality.* There is evidence of peer-like interactions between subject and parents who see each other as individuated people, but these interactions are either very recent or confined to safe or superficial areas.

5/6 The relationship is moving beyond the superficial sort of mutuality in some areas.

6 *Full Peer-Like Mutuality.*

interactions portion of the FRI has been transcribed and scored, and these scores were used for the analyses reported in this chapter.

FRI scoring was done by White and Costos, who independently rated each of the protocols for stage using a scoring manual (White and Costos, 1983). On a subsample of sixty protocols, the percentage of agreement for identical scores was .41, while the percentage for agreement within one-half stage was .82. Where there were differences, compromise scores were reached.

The Washington University Sentence Completion Test. Underlying Loevinger's (1966) thirty-six-item sentence completion test is the assumption that there are potentially seven stages of ego development, each more complex than the preceding one. Although these stages form an invariant sequence, not all individuals proceed through all stages. The stage at which an individual stops in the sequence is expected to have implications for a number of aspects of ego development, including conscious preoccupations and interpersonal style. Responses to the thirty-six-sentence stems of Loevinger's test are used to determine the predominant or core level of ego development characteristic of the respondent. Although arguing for the need for further construct validation of the Loevinger measure, Hauser (1976) reports good interscorer reliability. Hauser warns against expecting linear relations between ego development stages and other variables. To determine the extent to which Loevinger is correct in assuming that the stages correspond to a range of character types, we need, according to Hauser, stage-specific studies — that is, studies designed to determine the correlates of particular Loevinger stages. In the Family Relationships Project, we are both administering the Washington University Sentence Completion Test (WUSCT) longitudinally and determining the conceptual and empirical overlap between Loevinger's measure and our own.

Table 2 summarizes the conceptual parallels between Loevinger's ego development stages and White's relationship stages. Crucial to our data analyses is the assumption that the achievement of Loevinger's stage I-4, which marks the beginning of the ability to take a third-person perspective, is necessary but not sufficient for achievement of FRI stage 3, which is characterized by the individual's ability to show some perspective on the parent. We reasoned that some nonspecific perspective-taking ability would precede the ability to apply that perspective to emotion-laden personally involving relationships with parents. We did not predict a linear relationship between the two measures beyond FRI stage 3, because at that point further progress in family relationships stage requires the subject to view the parent as moving towards recognition and acceptance of the subject as an individual adult. We assume there may be cases where the individual ego development of the subject proceeds but where either the relationship with the parent is "stuck" because of parental characteristics or the relationship is perceived as stuck because of the way in which the subject views the parents.

The WUSCT protocols were scored by Costos, who attended ego development workshops at both Washington University and Harvard University. To assess the reliability of this scoring, a second rater, self-trained from

Table 2. Conceptual Overlap Between Loevinger and FRI Stages

Loevinger Stages	Family Relationship Interview Stages
Self-Protective Stage	1 *Individuation Stage*
Concern with staying out of trouble and in control	Independence
First-person perspective	Egocentric point of view
Good-bad dichotomizing	Right-wrong orientation
I-3 *Conformist Stage*	2 *Individuation Plus Perspective on Relationship Stage*
Interest in other's point of view	Attempts to understand parents but in stereotypic terms and only in reference to self
Pleasing others	
Conformist values	
Lack of introspection	
I-4 *Conscientious Stage*	3 *Individuation Plus Perspective on Parents Stage*
Ability to take third-person perspective	Ability to put self in parents' shoes
Sense of motives	Sense of motives for parent behavior
Self-evaluated standards	Parents seen as separate individuals

the scoring manual, scored a subsample of thirty protocols. When the second rater's total protocol ratings (TPRs) were compared with Costos's TPRs, the Spearman correlation coefficient was .81. In addition, item rating percent agreements between raters were calculated for eighteen of thirty-six sentence stems. Full stage agreement ranged from .50 to .80, with a mean of .62, while agreement within one-half stage ranged from .73 to .97, with a mean of .83.

The Speisman Part-Conflicts Scale. The Speisman Part-Conflicts Scale (SPCS) is an objective measure of Erikson's ego identity construct. The scale is made up of seven subscales designed to reflect the residuals (named *part-conflicts* by Gallatin, 1975) of Erikson's psychosocial stages of development. The inventory consists of 101 items, which the respondent is asked to rate as true or false. Here are two representative items: "When planning something, I don't really like others giving me their opinions regardless of who they might be." "Many of the arguments or quarrels I get into are over matters of principle."

The internal consistency for the total scale was found to be acceptable (alpha = .91, $n = 94$) as was the internal consistency (Hoyt range was .69 to .84) for all but subscales 3 and 6. Test-retest reliability was .72 for the total scale. A preliminary effort at construct validation was also promising, with statistically significant correlations in predicted directions found with measures of anxiety, self-esteem, ego control, and social desirability. The sample in our study took a modified version of the instrument consisting of ninety-seven items, which overlapped 95 percent with the previous item pool.

Procedures. Project participants were recruited through advertisements in newspapers, on the radio, and on bulletin boards in a variety of supermarkets and similar establishments. Individuals interested in the project mailed a brief form with their telephone number to project staff, who then called them to provide them with further details about project goals and procedures. Questionnaire packets, which included detailed informed consent forms, were mailed in advance of the interview date to all respondents who agreed to participate.

All subjects participated in tape-recorded individual interviews with a trained interviewer of their own sex in the Boston University Psychology Department. They received $5 an hour up to a maximum of $25 for their involvement. As part of the informed consent procedures, it was made clear to subjects that they were being asked to participate in a three-year project and that they would be contacted again in subsequent years for further participation. As part of the same informed consent process, we asked participants for permission to send a questionnaire version of the Family Relationships Interview to their parents. If subjects agreed, they provided us with parent addresses.

Results

In our sample of 156 subjects, stage scores for relationship with mother ranged from stage 1 to stage 4/5 (in transition from stage 4 to stage 5); scale scores ranged from 1 to 8. (The mothers of three subjects were deceased. Consequently, the descriptive statistics for relationship with mother were calculated only for 153 subjects.) Table 3 presents the results of a one-way analysis of variance in which family relationship stage score with mother was examined in relationship to sex, age, and marital status. The average scale score for women (4.65) was significantly higher than the average scale score for men (3.91; $F = 7.03$, $p < .009$). Stage scores on the Washington University Sentence Completion Test ranged from delta to I-5, with 125 of 156 subjects (80 percent) scoring at Loevinger's stages I-3/4 and I-4. There were no statistically significant sex differences in ego stage. Finally, total scores on the Speisman Part-Conflicts Scale ranged from 125 to 165. The mean scores were 148.9 for the women and 151.6 for the men ($F = 2.70$, $p < .10$). Unfortunately, we had SPCS total scores for only 112 subjects. Consequently, all the regression analyses reported in the next section were computed on this sample of 112 subjects.

Regression Analyses. For the purposes of the multiple regression analyses, only the FRI score with mother was used as the dependent variable, because preliminary analyses revealed the pattern of scores with mother to be more clear-cut than the pattern with father. Marital status (1 = single, 2 = married without children, 3 = married with children) was always entered first into the hierarchical regression equation, followed by the total score from the Speisman Part-Conflicts measure. The TPR score from Loevinger's sentence completion measure was entered last.

Table 3. Mean Scores and Analysis of Variance Results for Family Relationships Interview Scale Score with Mother by Age, Sex, and Marital Status

	Mean Scale Scores[a]					
			Age			
Marital	22-year-olds		24-year-olds		26-year-olds	
Status	Women	Men	Women	Men	Women	Men
Single	3.22	3.50	3.20	3.40	4.90	4.67
Married, without Children	3.89	4.00	5.00	4.80	6.10	4.00
Married, with Children			5.00	3.33	5.90	3.60

[a] The mothers of three subjects are deceased. The total number of mother scores for the sample of 156 is 153.

Analysis of Variance Results

Source of Variation	Mean Square	Degrees of Freedom	F Value	Significance of F Value
Main Effects	13.98	5	5.89	.0005
Age	12.57	2	5.29	.006
Sex	16.69	1	7.03	.009
Marital Status	12.68	2	5.34	.006

The regression of relationship with mother on marital status, Speisman Part-Conflicts score, and Loevinger TPR score yielded no statistically significant findings in the male sample. In contrast, both marital status and Speisman score were significant predictors of the women's relationship with their mothers (cumulative $r^2 = .34$, $p < .001$). Moreover, the Speisman Part-Conflicts score provided a significant increment to the variability accounted for by marital status (F change $= 10.32$, $p < .002$).

Although previous research with males suggests that the twenty-two- to twenty-six-year-old age group is fairly homogenous, we decided to add age as the first predictor variable in our regression equations. Age contributed nothing to the regression equation for males ($r^2 = .00$). However age was a significant predictor of relationship with mother ($F = 24.50$, $r^2 = .30$, $p < .001$) in women — and without cancelling out the independent effects due to marital status (F change $= 4.92$, $p < .03$) and Speisman Part-Conflicts score (F change $= 8.69$, $p < .005$). Indeed, the regression equation consisting of age, marital status, and Speisman Parts-Conflicts scores accounted for 44 percent of the variance in women's Family Relationships Interview scores with mother. Loevinger scores did not add a significant increment to the regression equation.

Ego Development and Family Relationships: Additional Analyses. Given that we had not predicted a linear relationship between ego development and family relationship stage score with mother, it seemed important to examine the relationship with a more appropriate statistical technique than regression analysis. Thus, we decided to use chi-square tests to examine our assumption that a Loevinger ego development score of 3/4 (indicating some movement towards a third-person perspective) was necessary but not sufficient for a family relationship score of 3 (indicating some perspective on the parent). Of seventy-eight subjects who received a relationship with mother score of 3 or higher, only four (5 percent) had a Loevinger score lower than stage 3/4.

Because only fourteen subjects scored lower than Loevinger stage 3/4, we continued our comparison of ego development and family relationship stage scores by regrouping the ego development scores into two categories — one that grouped stage I-3/4 and lower ($N = 73$), and one that grouped stage I-4 and higher ($N = 83$) — and by splitting the family relationship stage scores into two groups — stage 2/3 or lower ($N = 78$), and stage 3 or higher ($N = 78$). Chi-square analyses revealed that family relationships stage scores with mother at stage 3 and higher ($X^2 = 3.71$, $df = 1$, $p < .05$) were more likely to have ego development scores at stage 4 and higher. However, when these analyses were broken down by sex and repeated, the relationship was not statistically significant.

Discussion

Given the conceptual framework underlying the present research project, the sex differences in patterns of relationships among variables are of utmost interest. However, before we discuss these different patterns and their potential meaning, we would like to consider further the overall sex difference in family relationship stage score.

First, while the difference between men and women in family relationship stage is highly significant statistically, it is by no means enormous. The average stage score for women was stage 3, which indicates that women generally had perspective on their mothers as separate people. The average stage score for men was 2/3, indicating that men tended to see their mothers primarily in relationship to themselves but that they were moving toward perspective on their mothers as individuals in their own right. Contrast these statements by two of our subjects. (We have made minor changes to ensure confidentiality.) A young woman said: "I am understanding her more now than I ever did before. I have started to understand that I had to stop blaming her for everything in my life. I felt she had been a lousy parent. Now, I'm more understanding that my mother is a person and that she has her own problems and her own life. . . which I wasn't understanding of before. I accepted her as a mother — but she actually is a human being, and as an individual she had personality, and she had good days and bad days. I only saw her as a mother until recently." Note the difference in perspective expressed by a young man: "I have noticed things that I never knew before. My wife will ask me questions about my mother. If you asked me a question like, Where did she grow up? I never knew that. . . . I never thought to ask . . . my mother . . . tells us a situation between her and her father and makes it bigger than it really was. I never knew that until I left home and became married. . . . Maybe that . . . it's finally that I listened to these stories. But, I've noticed things about my mother that I've never noticed before."

While the average stage difference between males and females is moderate, the differential pattern of stage development across age and marital status is rather dramatically different for the two sexes. The twenty-six-year-old married women not only make it clear that they can see the world through their mother's eyes and not only make inferences about the psychological bases underlying their mother's behavior, but they also describe their mothers as engaging in mutual perspective taking—that is, as acknowledging the separateness and maturity of their daughters. This kind of perspective is generally not found in the twenty-two-year-old women, whether married or single, but there is some evidence for it in the twenty-four-year-old married women. In contrast, the twenty-six-year-old men, whether single or married, do not differ from the twenty-two- and twenty-four-year-old men. At all three ages, the emphasis is on individuation and on the parents as parents, not as separate individuals.

What is most remarkable is not the differences in perspective on mother but the overall sex differences in patterns of relationship among variables. Our expectation that psychosocial development would be related to family relationships stage was confirmed for women but not for men. Similarly, a relationship between the acquisition of an adult social role status (marriage, parenthood) was related to family relationship stage in women but not in men. What do these sex differences mean? Is the proposed sequence of steps in adult relationship development—that is, from individuation to perspective to peer-like mutuality—valid for women but not for men? Are individual and relationship development more tightly interrelated in women than they are in men? That is, do family interactions influence individual development differently in men than in women? And conversely, do differences in levels of individual psychological development affect family relationship development differently as a function of sex? We have no conclusive answers to such questions at this time, but we do believe that a number of possible explanations are worth exploring.

One possibility is that differential socialization experiences make an understanding of the perspective of others a more valued achievement for females than it is for males. There is already evidence that our society associates agency or autonomy more with the male sex role and communion or relatedness more with the female sex role. Both boys and girls must deal with issues of individuation during adolescence if they are to become mature and independent adults. After adolescence, women may use their entrance into adult roles to help them gain perspective on people with whom they have had very close relationships—that is, on their parents. In contrast, men may use their entrance into adult roles to confirm their autonomy, both to themselves and to their parents.

It is also possible that sex role socialization experiences make it more difficult for men, both as subjects and as interviewers, to talk about relationships. If this is the case, the young men in our sample may have a more fully-developed perspective on their mothers than the interviews make apparent. However, this possibility seems less likely to us than the previous one: Many young men talked a great deal about their relationships, but they placed a strong emphasis on the extent to which they were grown up and independent and respected for their independence by their parents.

Clearly this first cross-sectional analysis of data raises as many questions as it answers. To increase our understanding of how relationships with parents change over time and in relation to individual development and role status changes, an examination of longitudinal data will be crucial. We hope that, even in the two-year span between our first and third assessments of our young adult subjects, there will be enough change to allow us to determine the stability across time of the sex differences that we have discovered, the validity of the stage sequence posited for family relationships, and the potentially bidirectional influences between individual and relationship development, at least in women.

References

Bengston, V. L., and Black, K. D. "Solidarity Between Parents and Children: Four Perspectives on Theory Development." Paper presented at the National Council on Family Relations Theory Development Workshop, October 1973.

Block, J. H. "Conceptions of Sex Role: Some Cross-Cultural and Longitudinal Perspectives." *American Psychologist,* 1973, *28,* 512–526.

Cox, R. O. *Youth into Maturity: A Study of Men and Women in the First Ten Years After College.* New York: Mental Health Materials Center, 1970.

Douvan, E., and Adelson, J. *The Adolescent Experience.* New York: Wiley, 1966.

Erikson, E. H. "The Problems of Ego Identity." *Journal of the American Psychoanalytic Association,* 1956, *4,* 56–121.

Erikson, E. H. "Identity and the Life Cycle." *Psychological Issues,* 1959, *1,* (entire issue).

Gallatin, J. *Adolescence and Individuality.* New York: Harper & Row, 1975.

Gould, R. L. "The Phases of Adult Life: A Study in Developmental Psychology." *American Journal of Psychiatry,* 1972, *129* (5), 521–531.

Hauser, S. T. "Loevinger's Model and Measure of Ego Development: A Critical Review." *Psychological Bulletin,* 1976, *83,* 928–955.

Hill, R., Foote, N., Aldens, J., Carlson, R., and Macdonald, R. *Family Development in Three Generations.* Cambridge, Mass.: Schenkman, 1970.

Hinde, R. "On Describing Relationships." *Journal of Child Psychology and Psychiatry and Allied Disciplines,* 1976, *17,* 1–19.

Karpel, M. "Individuation: From Fusion to Dialogue." *Family Process,* 1976, *15,* 65–82.

Keniston, K. *Young Radicals: Notes on Committed Youth.* New York: Harcourt Brace and World, 1968.

Keniston, K. *Youth and Dissent: The Rise of the New Opposition.* New York: Harcourt Brace Jovanovich, 1971.

Klein, D. M., Jorgensen, S. R., and Miller, B. C. "Research Methods and Developmental Reciprocity in Families." In R. M. Lerner and G. B. Spanier (Eds.), *Child Influences on Marital and Family Interaction: A Life Span Perspective.* New York: Academic Press, 1978.

Levinger, G., and Raush, H. L. *Close Relationships: Perspectives on the Meaning of Intimacy.* Amherst: University of Massachusetts Press, 1977.

Levinson, D. J. *The Seasons of a Man's Life.* New York: Ballantine Books, 1978.

Loevinger, J. "The Meaning and Measurement of Ego Development." *American Psychologist,* 1966, *21,* 195–206.

Loevinger, J. *Ego Development: Conceptions and Theories.* San Francisco: Jossey-Bass, 1976.

Marcia, J. C. "Identity in Adolescence." In J. Adelson (Ed.), *Handbook of Adolescent Psychology.* New York: Wiley-Interscience, 1980.

Matteson, D. R. *Adolescence Today: Sex Roles and the Search for Identity.* Homewood, Ill.: Dorsey Press, 1975.

Newman, B. M., and Newman, P. R. *Development Through Life: A Psychosocial Approach.* Homewood, Ill.: Dorsey Press, 1975.

Ryder, R. G., Kafka, J. S., and Olson, D. H. "Separating and Joining Influences in Courtship and Early Marriage." *American Journal of Orthopsychiatry,* 1971, *41,* 450–464.

Speisman, J. C., White, K. M., Costos, D., Houlihan, J., and Imbasciati, C. "An Objective Instrument for Assessment of Erikson's Developmental Conflicts." Paper presented at the American Psychological Association meetings, Anaheim, Calif., August 1983.

Sussman, M. B. "Relations of Adult Children with Their Parents in the United States." In R. M. Lerner and G. B. Spanier (Eds.), *Child Influences on Marital and Family Interaction: A Life Span Perspective.* New York: Academic Press, 1978.

White, K., and Costos, D. "Scoring Manual for Family Relationships Interview Stages." Unpublished manuscript, 1983.

Kathleen M. White is associate professor of Psychology at Boston University. Her major research forcus is the family.

Joseph C. Speisman is professor of psychology at Boston University. His interests are in adolescent and young adult development, identity, and stress coping.

Daryl Costos is project director of the Family Relationships Project.

Adolescents' social behavior and empathy are both related
to the family's conception of the social world.

Family Paradigm and
Adolescent Social Behavior

David Reiss
Mary Ellen Oliveri
Karen Curd

A whole series of studies on the relationship between family process and adolescent development is beginning to emerge. Several of these studies are described in this volume. Two distinct strategies for approaching the problem can now be defined. First, investigators who are interested primarily in adolescence examine the social milieu of youngsters for forces that promote or impede their development. This can be called the up-from-adolescence strategy. Second, investigators whose primary interest is in large social systems, including the family, regard adolescent development as a product or manifestation—one among many—of the operation of these larger systems. This can be called down-from-society strategy. In this chapter, we summarize some of our own work that adopts the second strategy. However, a comprehensive approach to the study of family process and adolescence will, we believe, have to encompass both approaches. To begin our own efforts in that direction, we will present some new data from a study on family process and empathy in early adolescence. First, however, we will expand on these two perspectives.

    As already noted, the up-from-adolescence approach begins with a primary concern for adolescents and their development. Investigators typically have a keen interest in and a sure grasp of the underlying personality structures and their evolution and transformation through adolescence. A particu-

H. D. Grotevant and C. R. Cooper (Eds.). *Adolescent Development in the Family.* New
Directions for Child Development, no. 22. San Francisco: Jossey-Bass, December 1983.

larly good example is the work of Hauser and others (in press). These authors have a primary concern with ego development in adolescence, and they have carefully adapted Loevinger's concepts and methods for assessing this as the cornerstone of their work. They search the family for factors that enable or constrain adolescent initiative and that on a deeper level promote or inhibit ego development. They treat the family as an environment—a relatively unstructured field of atmospherics, in which individual structure (adolescents' as well as adults') unfolds.

The down-from-society approach to analyzing the relationship between family process and adolescence begins with a primary concern about the operation of the larger social systems: larger-scale social and cultural systems or the family itself. One approach views the family as a dependent component in a nexus of large-scale social forces. In this view, social and cultural forces play the central role in defining the family as an institution: its boundaries, its values, its functions, and major attributes of its component roles. This perspective has shaped the work of the great role theorists, beginning with Linton (1945) and continuing to current empirical work on family roles by Nye (1976).

Another approach within the same frame views the family itself as a source of initiative, as functioning according to its own rules, and as much an agent of social change as responsive to social change. Although this perspective has its roots in the work of such philosopher–social scientists as Mead (1934) and Berger and Luckmann (1966), it has been fueled in the last two decades primarily by the family therapy movement. Shrewd clinical observers have noted extraordinary patterns in family life and have reinterpreted a broad range of individual behaviors as part of an integrated system of family function. In the case of adolescents, both normal and abnormal development is not simply influenced by family process. Adolescent behavior is actually an inseparable component of family process. This perspective focuses less on adolescence per se than it does on the family and on how the family engineers its own development, stabilization, dissolution, and transformations. It tries to identify the manifest and latent tasks of family life, and it attempts to distinguish among families according to their idiosyncratic views of the world and themselves as well as according to how they position themselves vis-a-vis other family and social organizations in their everyday world.

These two viewpoints are not distinguished by their adherence to a particular direction of causality relating family and adolescent phenomena. The term *down from society* is meant to embrace a sequence in intellectual history, not a causal sequence. Investigators who embrace this view have started with an articulated and sensitive grasp of underlying social or family structure and proceeded to adolescent phenomena which they tend to view as surface behaviors, not as reflecting enduring and complex underlying structures located within the adolescent. However, investigators in this tradition are quite prepared to recognize that family structure can be responsive to these characteristics as well as causative of them, even if the adolescent character-istics are not finely conceptualized. Likewise, investigators in the up-from-adolescence tradition do not invariably search for the effects of adolescence on the family. Typically, they are interested in just the reverse or in reciprocal effects. What distinguishes the two groups, then, is not the direction of effect that they posit but the quality of connection between the two sets of variables: family and adolescent. We have tried to capture this quality in the up-from-adolescence tradition by the metaphor of family as atmosphere. A comparable though contrasting metaphor for the down-from-society tradition is behavior in context. This metaphor means to convey that this tradition understands behavior only as part of a field or pattern of social forces.

Our own work has mainly been in the down-from-society tradition. Our primary concern has been to understand differences among families, par-ticularly in their styles of relating to the surrounding social community. We have conducted a series of studies of adolescent social behavior, one of which is summarized in this chapter. This study has served larger aims of studying the family: Adolescent behavior has been seen either as an expression of underly-ing family mechanisms or as part of those mechanisms. However, recognizing that we have concentrated on surface rather than on underlying features of adolescence, we have begun to turn our attention to the relationship between family phenomena and more enduring attributes of adolescents. In this chapter, we summarize a study relating family process to empathy in early adolescence. This study is an attempt to combine the features of both the down-from-society and the up-from-adolescence traditions. In short, we have two aims: first, to introduce the reader to our approach to studying families and what it has yielded about adolescence; second, to use this summary to explore further the ramifications of the two traditions linking family and adolescence.

Family Paradigm: An Analysis of the Family's Transactions with Its Social World

Our studies focus on how the family experiences its social world. We have been struck by the degree to which individual families differ in this regard, particularly in ambiguous and stressful situations. For example, some families are typically optimistic and confident in such situations. They have an abiding belief that the social world operates by patterned and discoverable principles, which can be mastered through exploration. In contrast, other families experience the social world as chaotic and unknowable. Rather than exploring ambiguous and stressful situations, these families retreat into a self-protective huddle.

Kuhn (1970) provides a useful metaphor for characterizing these beliefs of family life which we refer to as *family paradigms*. A family paradigm is the set of core assumptions, convictions, or beliefs that each family holds about its environment; these assumptions guide the family to sample certain segments of its world and ignore others. The evidence that we have collected thus far suggests that the life of each family is organized by an enduring paradigm that emerges in the course of family development. We have proposed that family paradigms can undergo profound alteration at times of severe family disorganization but that they otherwise persist for years and even for generations. They are manifest, however, in the fleeting fantasies and expectations shared by all members of the family and, even more important, in the routine action patterns of daily life.

The keystone of our group's research program on the family paradigm has been the laboratory study of family problem solving, where we have developed a large set of new techniques. Conceptually, however, our work builds on a foundation laid by others, including Kluckhohn and Strodtbeck (1960), Bion (1959), Hess and Handel (1959) and Wynne and others (1958).

One core hypothesis of our work is that a family's paradigm becomes clearly manifest in a special type of family problem-solving task. One task that we have used in many studies requires family members to sit separately in booths. Each family member must sort a deck of cards that bears series of letters into piles. Many families recognize that the cards can be grouped according to the sequential pattern of the letters. For example, PMSMSVK can be grouped with PMSMSMSMSVK, and PMSFK can be grouped with PMSS-SSSFK. In some phases of the task, family members can talk with one another on a telephone-like hookup; in others, they work alone.

Virtually every family in our testing situation is puzzled at first. Our description of the study — its aims and procedures — as well as the laboratory instructions are clear enough. But, every family seems to ask us, in its own way, Why are you doing this to us? What do these games really tell you about our family? At the core, our subject families face the central interpretive challenge of deciding what are the inherent potentials and possibilities in this strange situation. During all the years in which we have used procedures of this kind, it has been our impression that a family's approach to solving the puzzles that they present depends heavily on its own interpretation of what we as a research staff are trying to discover. No matter what we tell our families, they make their own determination and then seem to listen only to those parts of the explicit experimental instructions that fit this determination. Some families, of course, believe what we tell them and follow our experimental instructions to the letter. But, this also is an active, interpretive process on their part. They have determined that we can be trusted, whether or not we actually deserve such trust. The most crucial point here is that we can infer a family's view of us by objective measures of their problem-solving performance.

Families' performance in the card sort procedure differs along three distinct dimensions. A family high on configuration delves deep into the problem to discover its structure; its solutions are complex and patterned. At the other extreme, the solutions of families low on configuration are simple and superficial and show little evidence of a search for underlying patterns of connection among the elements of the puzzle. Our hypothesis is that high configuration families are not simply more skillful at problem solving than low configuration families but that high configuration families see the problem as soluble from the very start. Low configuration families feel that we have given them an insoluble problem.

A second way in which the families differ is the degree to which the efforts of each individual member are integrated into a common strategy during the part of the task when the family works together. We call this dimension coordination. Members in high coordination families are careful to pay attention to what the others are doing. There is often much discussion and serious attempts to reconcile differing views, and as a consequence each member's actual solution is similar or identical to that of other family members. In contrast, there is little integration of each member's efforts in low coordination families. At the extreme, family members hardly talk to each other, and each member seems unaware of what the others are thinking or doing.

In the card sort procedure, families differ in yet a third way, which we call closure. Some families pick a solution early in the family portion of the task and stick with it through thick or thin. Other families seem willing to change their system in the light of new data. We have hypothesized that early closure families attach priority to their own traditions and past; in effect, the world is divided into categories shaped by the family's immersion in its own history. Delayed closure families see each experience as novel and unrelated to them and their past, and they search for what is unique in each new setting.

The studies described in this chapter explore two dimensions: configuration and coordination. If we divide any sample at the median of these two dimensions, we create a four-category typology. We call families high on both configuration and coordination *environment-sensitive*. Members of these families organize cooperatively to detect and investigate the full range of subtle nuances in their social and informational environment. Families high on coordination but low on configuration are called *consensus-sensitive*. Members of these families are attuned primarily to the thoughts and feelings of one another. Indeed, their subtle sensitivity to one another screens out a broad range of experiences and patterns in the outer world, a world that seems hazy at best and formless and menacing at worst. Families high on configuration but low on coordination are called *achievement-sensitive*. Members of these families do not see themselves as part of a group but as individuals operating on their own to secure success in a tough but masterable world. Finally, families low on both configuration and coordination are termed *distance-sensitive*. Members are isolated in a private world, partially or completely oblivious to the experience of others. The outside world of people, places, events, and things is lived in but neither explored nor understood.

A long series of laboratory and field studies has explored aspects of this model. First, the psychometic properties of the card sorting procedure were investigated. Test-retest reliability is high (Oliveri and Reiss, 1983), and scores are not influenced by such variables as social class, level of education, individual intelligence (Oliveri and Reiss, 1981b), or perceptual style (Reiss and Oliveri, in press). The dimensions and typologies of family paradigm that the card sorting procedure delineates correlate well with more direct measures of family experience, and it has predicted a broad range of families' responses to their social environment: to psychiatric hospitalization (Reiss and others, 1980; Costell and others, 1981; Costell and Reiss, 1982), to chronic illness (Reiss and others, 1983), to relationships with friends and extended kin (Oliveri and Reiss, 1981a; Reiss and Oliveri, 1983), and to coping with stress. Specific findings have been replicated in work by our group (Reiss and Salzman, 1973) and by groups in this country (Davis and others, 1980) and abroad (Shulman and Klein, 1982).

Down from Society: Family Paradigm and Adolescent Sociability

In this section, we describe selected findings from a previous study (Reiss and others, 1980) that viewed adolescent behavior as an integral component of family functioning and that examined the connection between paradigm, as assessed from problem-solving behavior, and family members' social behavior. The general thesis guiding the study was that the enduring assumptions that families hold about the social world—their paradigms—are manifested in the types of bonds that they form with individuals and groups outside the family. The findings selected for presentation here refer to the issue of how dimensions of family paradigms relate to variation in adolescents' social interactions. The paradigm dimensions of configuration and coordination and their interaction were most salient in pointing up such variation.

The study concerned families' relationships with a family-oriented treatment program for psychiatrically disturbed adolescents. The process of families' engagement in treatment was the prime focus of examination. The study was conducted in an inpatient psychiatric treatment unit, and many of the measures of treatment process examined were obtained by observing family members' interactions with other families and staff in a multiple-family discussion group (MFG) held on a weekly basis over a period of months. As Reiss and others (1980) have described, several aspects of families' prominence and conspicuousness in the MFG, the nature of boundaries between family and other group members, and families' sense of engagement with the group were measurable, and these constituted salient markers both of families' investment in treatment and of their potential for gaining benefit from it. Of the measures examined, those tapping boundary issues between family members and the other members of the MFG were most useful in highlighting the connection between paradigm and adolescents' social behavior. Measures of engagement with the group were also helpful in amplifying distinctions found among adolescents and their families.

Two kinds of measures tapped boundary issues. First, once each month, family members completed sociometric questionnaires that asked which individuals in the group they most liked, least liked, most knew, and least knew. We were interested in the extent to which subjects would choose their own family rather than other members of the group in response to these questions. Second, detailed records were kept of seating patterns in the group, and measurements were made of the extent to which family members chose to sit close to one another or to disperse in the group. On both measures, adolescent responses or behavior contributed most strongly to the paradigm-related differences that we found. That is, the differences in adolescents', not in parents', within-family or extra-family sociometric choices were particularly salient, and it was the distance between the adolescent and his or her parents, not the distance between parents, that was the major contributor to variation on the seating measure. Thus, in this summary of findings, we refer to these measures as reflecting adolescent autonomy in interaction with the MFG. Measures of engagement for parents included regularity of attendance at the group meetings. (Adolescents, being inpatients, were less free to be absent.) The index of engagement for adolescents was cooperation in regularly completing a questionnaire that tapped feelings about the group and its process; this index of engagement has been cross-validated (Koran and Costell, 1966).

Analyses of association of problem-solving dimensions with both autonomy measures — sociometric choices and seating measures — indicated lower levels of adolescent-parent autonomy in consensus-sensitive and achievement-sensitive families than in distance-sensitive and environment-sensitive families. The relatively low degree of autonomy as a characteristic of consensus-sensitive families is consistent with the conceptualization of these families as placing a primacy on family unity at the expense of exploration of the environment. That the same level would be observed in achievement-sensitive families, however, sharply contrasts with their problem-solving performance, which suggests an emphasis on independent exploration and mastery of the enviroment.

Two considerations, however, suggest that this contradiction may be more apparent than it is real. First, it is plausible that the need of these family members to demonstrate their own circumscribed areas of competence demands that they pay close attention to one another in order to assure that the individual achievement of one is not undercut or overlapped by that of another; thus the close proximity in seating patterns. Such a tendency to closely monitor one another, if it exists, may have been exaggerated in the inpatient unit, since family members were operating in the same social field; that is, they could not interact with the MFG on their own, since other family members were always present. Second, the treatment program itself focused on treatment of the family as a group. It emphasized open communication, group solidarity, and the primacy of the family unit. Families oriented toward individual exploration of the environment may have been ill equipped to use their typical modes of interaction in a setting that placed such a high value on the unity of the family group. Thus, the high number of within-family sociometric choices in achievement-sensitive families, which were primarily most-like choices, may have marked their inhibitions about forming relationships with other group members, because their characteristic style of relating to the social world was counteracted by the group norms. Consistent with this interpretation was the additional finding that adolescents in achievement-sensitive families tended to demonstrate a low sense of engagement and investment in the group.

In environment-sensitive and distance-sensitive families, adolescent-parent autonomy was relatively high: Within-family sociometric choices were low, and adolescents tended in their seating patterns to disperse away from their parents (or parents from the adolescents) and into the group. We feel that the reasons for this finding are quite different for these two groups of families. Environment-sensitive families tend to work collectively in order to master the problem to be solved. Members of distance-sensitive families appear to be pessimistic both about the potential for benefiting from one another's input and about whether the problem can in fact be solved. Thus, the high autonomy demonstrated by adolescents in environment-sensitive families may have reflected the family's sense that exploration of the environment is vital if the family as a group is to grapple with it effectively. In distance-sensitive families, however, it seems more likely that the high autonomy demonstrated by adolescents reflects members' lack of strong connection with one another. Consistent with these views are findings of distance-sensitive and environment-sensitive families' levels of engagement with the MFG. Adolescents and their parents in distance-sensitive families showed the least engagement of the four types of families, while members of environment-sensitive families exhibited some of the highest levels of engagement. Clinical observations of these families blind to their typing by laboratory performance (Costell and Reiss, 1982) have highlighted the same difference. Parents in distance-sensitive families were described as befuddled and depleted and adolescents as depressed and self-destructive. In environment-sensitive families, clinical portrayals emphasize members as being gregarious, direct, and honest; fathers in such families as being striking for their involvement with their children; and adolescents in such families as being open, assertive, aggressive, and well integrated into their group of adolescent peers.

Taking the down-from-society approach, we have interpreted findings from this study by considering adolescent social behavior as an understandable outgrowth of the family's paradigm. That is, the differences found among adolescents in the four groups of families regarding their behavior vis-à-vis the MFG can be understood as an expression or manifestation of distinct differences in families' underlying conceptions of the social world. Elsewhere, (Reiss, 1981), we have proposed a cycle hypothesis that permits us to take these speculations one step further. The cycle hypothesis proposes in part that the type of links formed by any family member with the outside social world not only expresses the family's paradigm but serves to stabilize it. To restate this point in other terms, adolescent social behavior, along with social behavior in other family members, serves to maintain the family's particular conception of social reality. Thus, the high levels of engagement with the MFGs by adolescents in environment-sensitive families may serve to confirm these families' conception of the outside world as understandable and masterable. Likewise, the isolated retreat from the MFG by adolescents in distance-sensitive families may serve to confirm or reinforce the belief of these families that they cannot engage the social environment effectively.

Combining Two Traditions: Family Paradigm and Empathy in Early Adolescence

In the study just described, we focused on relatively narrowly defined adolescent behavior. We argued that an adolescent's social behavior — his or her autonomy from his parents and his or her engagement in cohesive groups outside the family — is an understandable reflection of the family's paradigm. Beyond that, we speculated that the adolescent's behavior may actually reinforce or stabilize the family's paradigm. In this section, we present previously unpublished data concerning the relationship of paradigm to adolescent variables of a very different quality. We report the results of a study comparing the family's paradigm to the level of empathy in forty-one seventh-grade girls and boys. Data suggest that empathy is a structured assembly of skills and motivations (Feffer and Gourevitch, 1960; Flavell and others, 1968; Katz, 1963; and Weinstein, 1971) that emerges clearly in twelve- or thirteen-year-olds (Flavell and others, 1968) and that serves as an enduring attribute useful for distinguishing among early and late adolescents as well as adults (Adams and others, 1979; Chandler, 1973; Eisenberg-Berg and Mussen, 1978). Two fundamental capacities inherent in empathy are a high level of sensitivity to subtle interpersonal cues and skill in taking the role of another — that is, an ability to sense the perspectives, outlooks, and needs of another. Thus, it seemed reasonable to suppose the environment-sensitive families would contain empathic adolescents, since the environment-sensitive paradigm expresses both high degrees of sensitivity to a broad range of social stimuli and high levels of sensitivity among family members to one another.

However, empathy is not the same kind of variable as the adolescent social behaviors on which we focused in the preceding section. It comes much closer to being a true internal structure — an enduring attribute with many surface behavioral manifestations — and it reflects innate capacities and a variety of experiences in the adolescent's past. Because of its interiority and endurance, empathy cannot simply be regarded as family atmosphere. A different relational metaphor is required. We suggest the notion of component. By component, we mean to suggest an image of a large and complex machine that cannot operate without its major components. Adolescent empathy is a component of a family machine, some of whose properties are encompassed by the notion of paradigm. Empathy can be considered a submechanism that is crucial for the operation of the whole. The concept of empathy as a submechanism also allows us to think of bidirectional influences between family and adolescent. For example, it seems plausible that an environment-sensitive family depends on the presence of empathic adolescents to maintain its particular conception of itself in the world. That is, while the family may have little influence in shaping empathy in its adolescents, it may still be highly responsive to this attribute once it emerges in response to a variety of nonfamily factors. However, it seems equally plausible to argue that, owing to its dependence on enduring empathy in its members, the family has acquired the capacity to encourage or structure the development of empathy over time.

The metaphor of the machine and its components is meant to emphasize qualities of the nature of the relationship between family and adolescent process that the metaphors of family as atmosphere and behavior in context do not convey. It differs from these other metaphors, first, in respect to time and history. Whatever the influence of paradigm on empathy or the reverse, these are likely to extend over long periods of time; neither is likely to change the other quickly.

The second way in which the machine metaphor differs from the other two concerns the conceptual space between the two sets of variables. In the up-from-adolescence approach, the investigator picks family variables because they are conceptually apposite to the adolescent structure of interest. Theory can quite rationally specify that the family variable influences or responds to the adolescent characteristics directly, not through a large number of intervening processes. This is less true of such variables as paradigm and empathy. Even if longitudinal studies could carefully map out the causal direction relating these two variable sets, we would still be required to explore a complex intervening mechanism. The variable sets that we have chosen are structurally central to family and adolescent process. Their conceptual apposition to one another is less secure. In the case of empathy, then, the concept of component is meant to emphasize that empathy may be crucial to the working of the family machine. However, its exact mechanical fit with the overall intricate mechanism remains to be specified.

The third way in which the machine metaphor differs from the other two involves the magnitude of influence of one variable set on the other. This influence is likely to be relatively small. Because component and machine are responsive to such a broad range of variables over time, neither can explain the other adequately. Here, the concept of component emphasizes that, although both component and overall mechanism can be crucial to one another once they are linked, their present interrelationships may be unrelated to the history of their construction. That is, once component and machine are meshed, each is crucial to the operation of the other, but the machine cannot be said to have "manufactured" the component or vice versa.

In our study of paradigm and empathy, our sample consisted of forty-one seventh-grade students aged twelve to thirteen, and their natural parents. Forty-one other children were recruited for an accessory sample, as we explain later. Parents were in good physical health and under age sixty, and their occupations and education were distributed across the top three categories of the Hollingshead-Redlich scale. No subjects, adults or children, had a history of psychiatric treatment, and all were fluent in English. The sample was divided into four groups, using the dimensions of configuration and coordination, according to their performance on the card sort procedure. Eight variables were used to check on the comparability of fathers, mothers, and children in these four groups: parental intelligence, child intelligence, parental age, occupational rating of chief wage earner, mother's education, father's education, parental salary, and the ordinal position of the child tested. Of a total of fifty-six comparisons (main effects of configuration, coordination, and sex of child and interactions), only one was significant at the .01 level (configuration × sex interaction for child intelligence), and four were significant at the .10 level (configuration × sex for mothers; sex for father's education; configuration × sex for parental salary and sex for ordinal position). Although these variables had small and generally nonsignificant associations with the measures of empathy, an analysis of covariance was performed to assess possible confounding.

Three different measures were used to assess empathy, the dependent variable. The first was the Fry communication task (Fry, 1961, 1966). A subject, the speaker, was paired with a listener from the accessory sample. The pairing was based on a sociogram that assured that speaker and listener knew each other well but were not best friends. Both speaker and listener were presented with an array of complex figures. On the speaker's card, one figure was marked with an X. The speaker was asked to describe this figure clearly enough to allow the listener to select the same figure from the array on his or her card. The score was based both on the speed and accuracy of the listener's response and on coder ratings of two attributes of the speaker's communication: presence of adequate information (interrater reliability = .89) and overall clarity (interrater reliability = .69). The second measure was the Dymond test of interpersonal perception (Dymond, 1948, 1949, 1950; Dymond and others, 1952). This test paired the same speaker and listener, who were asked to rate self and the other (on a scale of 1 to 5) on ten bipolar traits, such as shy–self-confident, leader–follower, and excitable–calm. (All ten pairs were pretested to be fully comprehensible to seventh graders.) Further, the speaker was asked to rate the same ten items, first, as he or she thought the listener might have rated himself or herself; second, as he or she thought the listener had rated him or her. The speaker was scored for the accuracy of the last two judgments. The third measure was Hogan's self-report empathy scale (Hogan, 1972; Hogan and Henley, 1970). Its sixty-four items were drawn from the Minnesota Multiphasic Personality Inventory (MMPI) and the California Personality Inventory on the basis of their power to discriminate observer-rated socially acute and socially insensitive youngsters; seventh graders have been used specifically in validation samples. Despite different theoretical origins and substantially different approaches to measurement, empathy scores from the three measures correlate quite well: For Fry and Dymond, $r = .63$; for Fry and Hogan, $r = .48$; and for Dymond and Hogan, $r = .51$—all significant beyond the .01 level. Moreover, none of the three measures correlated with the child's intelligence.

The results, which are displayed in Table 1, are quite striking. The pattern of findings is the same for all three measures of empathy. The basic hypothesis that environment-sensitive paradigms would be associated with high empathy was confirmed only for girls. For boys, the reverse was true. The highest empathy was associated with distance-sensitive families and in general with low coordination. Examination of the simple main effects reveals that, for all three dependent variables, girls were more empathic than boys in high coordination families. Finally, a trend for boys associated high configuration with reduced empathy—an effect that reached significance only on the Dymond test. For girls, the reverse was true, since the effect reached significance only for high coordination families of females on the Dymond test. In sum, there was a striking and opposite effect of coordination and configuration for boys and girls: High coordination and, to a lesser extent, high configuration were associated with high empathy in girls, but the reverse was true for boys. It should be noted that there was no main effect due to sex on any measure. This is consistent with the literature on measures of empathy that focus on taking the other's perspective as in the Fry test and on perceiving others' affects as in the Dymond test (Hoffman, 1977). Girls are superior to boys only in the capacity to experience in themselves (not just to perceive) the affect experienced by others—a component of empathy that we did not assess in this study.

What explains these sex differences? Recent evidence and theory presented by Gilligan (1982) suggests that we may be seeing the interaction of cultural and family phenomena in our findings. Gilligan identifies a cultural script that distinguishes empathy and moral development in men and women. As boys develop, they organize their conception of morality around the curbing of aggression, learning principles to avoid hurting others and to allow each individual a fair chance to succeed on his own. Respect and sensitivity to others then becomes organized around clear, statable principles for assuring independence and autonomy. In contrast, development for girls is shaped by a norm that Gilligan calls the "ethic of caring." Girls struggle to resolve conflicts between selfishness and connectedness to others. Ethical dilemmas are not solved by abstract principles of avoiding harm and respect for others' autonomy. Solutions involve more situationally determined efforts to maintain relationships: to act while remaining embedded in a web of deeply felt ties with others. Thus, women's sensitivity to others is directed at reducing distances between self and others, not at maintaining them. Thus, we speculate, families

Table 1. Relationship Between Family Paradigm and Empathy in Forty-One Seventh Graders

| | | Z-Scores for Empathy Measures | | | Significant F Ratios | |
| | | Configuration | | | | |
Coordination	Sex	Low	High	ANOVA	ANCOVA	Simple Main Effects for ANOVA
				Fry Test		
High	Male	−.41	−1.21	$F_{CD \times sex} = 7.61***$	$F_{CD \times sex} 6.61**$	High CD: $F_{sex} = 4.93**$
	Female	.01	.55			
Low	Male	.51	.14			
	Female	−.04	−.72			
				Dymond Test		
		Low	High			
High	Male	−.05	−1.39	$F_{CD \times sex} = 4.89**$	$F_{CD \times sex} = 4.71**$	High CD: $F_{sex} = 3.35*$
	Female	−.39	−.78			High Females: $F_{C \times C} = 5.38**$
Low	Male	.78	.05	$F_{CF \times sex} = 3.54*$	$F_{CF \times sex} = 4.75**$	Low CD: $F_{CF} = 3.00*$
	Female	.37	−.49	$F_{C \times C \times sex} = 4.49**$	$F_{C \times C \times sex} = 4.75**$	Males: $F_{CF} = 3.01*$
				Hogan Test		
		Low	*High*			
High	Male	−.08	−1.18	$F_{CD \times sex} = 3.55*$	$F_{CD \times sex} = 3.55*$	High CD: $F_{sex} = 4.80**$
	Female	.25	.70			
Low	Male	.05	.02			
	Female	.07	−.30			

Note: CD = coordination; CF = configuration; $C \times C$ = configuration × coordination; $*p < .10$; $**p < .05$; $***p < .01$; ANCOVA covariates were child intelligence, mother's education, father's education, parental salary (total), and ordinal position of child tested.

90

with great interpersonal distance among members mesh with the development of an ethic of autonomy, a sensitivity to and respect for the personal and separate world of others, a sensitivity most appropriate — according to Gilligan's cultural script — for boys. In contrast, closely connected families mesh with a sensitivity to relationships in the service of maintaining intimate connections. It is this interpersonal sensitivity that the cultural script favors for girls. Of course, our findings from a single cross-sectional study cannot distinguish direction of causality. Families with empathic boys who are very sensitive and who seek separateness may be influenced as a group to adopt a low coordination paradigm. Likewise, families with empathic girls may be influenced to become high in coordination. Or, the reverse may be true: In order to maintain a particular paradigm, families may influence empathy in boys and girls differently to accommodate larger family aims and perceptions.

The two sets of findings presented here serve to highlight two different strategies for investigating family process and adolescence. The first study uses adolescent behavior as a window on family process. The second study examines how two stable structures — family paradigm and adolescent empathy — fit together. We have speculated that, in studies of the second type, relationships between family and adolescent variables will often be complex, and conceptualization and study of mediating variables will be required. Indeed, sex of child turned out to be just this kind of mediating variable.

How can these studies be related? A clear answer can be given only when we know more about the relationship between empathy and the types of adolescent behavior that we selected for study. The present data allow us to speculate that adolescent social behavior may be more malleable than empathy and thus that it may be immediately available to serve the larger aims of the family. For example, in another study of multiple family groups (Reiss and Costell, 1977), we have shown how finely tuned adolescent social participation is to parental levels of engagement in the group. Adolescents adjust their levels of participation on a minute-by-minute basis to match their parents' levels, and vice versa, even when the group divides into two distinct subgroups, with adolescents interacting with other adolescents and adults interacting with adults. Some psychiatric symptoms may also show this malleable responsiveness to larger family aims. In contrast, deeper adolescent structures, such as empathy, are not so easily summoned to serve the family cause. Rather, the process is slower and consists of measured piecing together of individual and family structure.

References

Adams, G. R., Schvaneveldt, J. D., and Jenson, G. O. "Sex, Age, and Perceived Competency as Correlates of Empathic Ability in Adolescence." *Adolescence,* 1979, *14,* 811–818.
Berger, P. L., and Luckmann, T. *The Social Construction of Reality.* New York: Doubleday, 1966.

Bion, W. *Experience in Groups.* New York: Basic Books, 1959.

Chandler, M. J. "Egocentrism and Antisocial Behavior: The Assessment and Training of Social Perspective-Taking Skills." *Developmental Psychology,* 1973, *9,* 326-332.

Costell, R., and Reiss, D. "The Family Meets the Hospital: Clinical Presentations of a Laboratory-Based Family Typology." *Archives of General Psychiatry,* 1982, *39,* 443-448.

Costell, R., Reiss, D., Berkman, H., and Jones, C. "The Family Meets the Hospital: Predicting the Family's Perception of the Treatment Program from its Problem-Solving Style." *Archives of General Psychiatry,* 1981, *38,* 569-577.

Davis, P., Stern, D., Jorgenson, J., and Steier, F. *Typologies of the Alcoholic Family: An Integrated Systems Perspective.* Philadelphia: Wharton Applied Research Center, University of Pennsylvania, 1980.

Dymond, R. "A Preliminary Investigation of the Relation of Insight and Empathy." *Journal of Consulting Psychology,* 1948, *12,* 228-233.

Dymond, R. "A Scale for the Measurement of Empathic Ability." *Journal of Consulting Psychology,* 1949, *13,* 127-133.

Dymond, R. "Personality and Empathy." *Journal of Consulting Psychology,* 1950, *14,* 343-350.

Dymond, R. F., Hughes, A. S., and Raabe, V. L. "Measurable Changes in Empathy with Age." *Journal of Consulting Psychology,* 1952, *16,* 202-206.

Eisenberg-Berg, N., and Mussen, P. "Empathy and Moral Development in Adolescence." *Developmental Psychology,* 1978, *14* (2), 185-186.

Feffer, M., and Gourevitch, S. "Cognitive Aspects of Role Taking in Children." *Journal of Personality,* 1960, *28,* 383-396.

Flavell, J. H., Botkin, P. T., Fry, C. L., Wright, J. W., and Jarvis, R. W. *The Development of Role Taking and Communication Skills in Children.* New York: Wiley, 1968.

Fry, C. L. "The Effects of Training in Communication and Role Perception on the Communicative Abilities of Children." Unpublished doctoral dissertation, University of Rochester, 1961.

Fry, C. L. "Training Children to Communicate as Listeners." *Child Development,* 1966, *37,* 675-685.

Gilligan, C. *In a Different Voice: Psychological Theory and Women's Development.* Cambridge, Mass.: Harvard University Press, 1982.

Hauser, S. T., Powers, S. I., Noam, G., Jacobson, A. M., Weiss, B., and Follansbee, D. J. "Familial Contexts of Adolescent Ego Development." *Child Development,* in press.

Hess, R. D., and Handel, G. *Family Worlds.* Chicago: University of Chicago Press, 1959.

Hoffman, M. L. "Sex Differences in Empathy and Related Behaviors." *Psychological Bulletin,* 1977, *84* (4), 712-722.

Hogan, R. "Development of an Empathy Scale." *Journal of Consulting and Clinical Psychology,* 1972, *33,* 307-316.

Hogan, R., and Henley, N. "A Test of the Empathy-Effective Communication Hypothesis." Report No. 84. Baltimore: Center for the Study of Social Organization of Schools, Johns Hopkins University, 1970.

Katz, R. *Empathy: Its Nature and Uses.* London: Free Press Glencoe, 1963.

Kluckhohn, F. R., and Strodtbeck, F. L. "Varieties in the Basic Values of Family Systems." In N. W. Bell and E. F. Vogel (Eds.), *A Modern Introduction to the Family.* Glencoe, Ill.: Free Press, 1960.

Koran, L. M., and Costell, R. "Early Termination from Group Psychotherapy." *International Journal of Group Psychotherapy,* 1966, *15,* 267-275.

Kuhn, T. S. *The Structure of Scientific Revolutions.* (2nd ed.) Chicago: University of Chicago Press, 1970.

Linton, R. *The Cultural Background of Personality.* New York: Appleton-Century-Crofts, 1945.

Mead, G. H. *Mind, Self, and Society.* Chicago: University of Chicago Press, 1934.
Nye, F. I. *Role Structure and Analysis of the Family.* Beverly Hills, Calif.: Sage, 1976.
Oliveri, M. E., and Reiss, D. "The Structure of Families' Ties to Their Kin: The Shaping Role of Social Construction." *Journal of Marriage and the Family,* 1981a, *43,* 391–407.
Oliveri, M. E., and Reiss, D. "A Theory-Based Empirical Classification of Family Problem-Solving Behavior." *Family Process,* 1981b, *20,* 409–418.
Oliveri, M. E., and Reiss, D. "Family Concepts and Their Measurements: Things Are Seldom What They Seem." Unpublished manuscript, 1983.
Reiss, D. *The Family's Construction of Reality.* Cambridge, Mass.: Harvard University Press, 1981.
Reiss, D., and Costell, R. "The Multiple Family Group as a Small Society: Family Regulation of Interaction Between Its Members and Nonmembers." *American Journal of Psychiatry,* 1977, *134,* 21–24.
Reiss, D., Costell, R., Jones, C., and Berkman, H. "The Family Meets the Hospital: A Laboratory Forecast of the Encounter." *Archives of General Psychiatry,* 1980, *37,* 141–154.
Reiss, D., Gonzalez, S., Wolin, S., Steinglass, P., and Kramer, N. "Family Process, Chronic Illness, and Death." Unpublished manuscript, 1983.
Reiss, D., and Oliveri, M. E., "The Family's Construction of Social Reality and Its Ties to Its Kin Network: An Exploration of Causal Direction." *Journal of Marriage and the Family,* 1983, *81,* 92.
Reiss, D., and Oliveri, M. E. "Sensory Experience and Family Process: Perceptual Styles Tend to Run in but Not Necessarily Run Families." *Family Process, 45,* in press.
Reiss, D., and Salzman, C. "The Resilience of Family Process: Effect of Secobarbital." *Archives of General Psychiatry,* 1973, *28,* 425–533.
Shulman, S., and Klein, M. M. "The Family and Adolescence: A Conceptual and Experimental Approach." *Journal of Adolescence,* 1982, *5,* 219–234.
Weinstein, E. "The Development of Interpersonal Competence." In D. Goslin (Ed.), *Handbook of Socialization Theory and Research.* Chicago: Rand McNally, 1971.
Wynne, L. C., Ryckoff, I. M., Day, J., and others. "Pseudomutuality in the Family Relations of Schizophrenics." *Psychiatry,* 1958, *21,* 205–220.

David Reiss is professor and director of the Division of Research in the Department of Psychiatry and Behavioral Sciences, George Washington University School of Medicine, Washington, D.C.

Mary Ellen Oliveri is associate research professor in the Department of Psychiatry and Behavioral Sciences, George Washington University School of Medicine, Washington, D.C.

Karen Curd is a psychologist with the Poway Unified Schools in California and a clinical child psychologist in Del Mar, California.

This chapter discusses and integrates the five preceding chapters and places them in context within the social sciences.

Social Construction of Adolescence by Adolescents and Parents

James Youniss

In an age when the human capacity for rationality is seriously under question and when individualism is being tempered with social responsibility, theories of adolescence promote the view that adolescents can, through the use of reason, come to an ordered and principled conception of reality. This theoretical posture shows disdain for scholarly analyses of society, demonstrates the consequences of abstracting adolescents out of society, or both. Perhaps these charges are too harsh. Perhaps psychological theorists do not mean that adolescents liberate themselves from the parent-child bond through recourse to self-reflective reasoning. But, a close reading of the literature on identity, morality, and ego development implies otherwise. Indeed, the generalization that cuts across theories is that to remain within the parental viewpoint and to conform to it is less than mature. To go beyond it because reasoning dictates is to enter the postconventional realm of maturity.

The work described in this volume constitutes a first step away from the position that has become a standard for psychological theories. The authors recognize that the parent-child bond can endure through the adolescent period. Development may consist not so much in breaking the bond as in transforming it and the persons within it. The authors also recognize that adolescents may not be so trusting of their own rationality that they fail to seek validation for their ideas from their parents. Positively, the authors attempt to

H. D. Grotevant and C. R. Cooper (Eds.). *Adolescent Development in the Family.* New
Directions for Child Development, no. 22. San Francisco: Jossey-Bass, December 1983.

demonstrate the point with samples of communicative interactions in which some episodes represent individualistic monologues, others illustrate unilateral influence, but many manifest attempts to achieve mutual understanding.

Of the several points made in this volume, these two and their associated implications are the focus of this chapter, which aims to provide an overview and to bring perspective to the five preceding chapters. While the focus selected may fall short of a broad view, it is justified insofar as it gives a coherent perspective to the work both in terms of content and with respect to other approaches to adolescence.

General Comments

The research reported in these chapters has multiple origins. One is standard theory, in which measures of adolescent development include identity exploration, role taking, and ego functioning. Another is family systems theory, in which triads rather than individuals are the basic units and family styles or patterns are thought to explain the behavior of the respective members. A third is open-minded empirical appraisal of communication, in which interactive data are used inductively to describe strategies of exchange. A fourth is communication theory, which places the premium on conversation insofar as it leads to consensus. A fifth is life span theory, which views parents as well as adolescents as operating according to stage-characteristic modes and which seeks to discern how their junction meshes or leads to discord.

For each of these points of origin, the authors of the chapters in this volume have sampled only some of the available constructs. It is likely that experts in any one of these domains will be dissatisfied with the result. However, the authors seem willing to accept such a charge, because it is obvious that they favor a many-sided over a single narrow approach. For example, specialists in interactive data may attack the coding systems that break sequences of exchange into categories or classes of discrete acts (Gottman and Ringland, 1981). The authors can bear such criticisms because their data represent initial phases of projected long-term research programs and because their present goal is to see whether family communication patterns can predict indicators of development in adolescents.

Dissatisfaction may also be felt by critics who ask how the authors hope to speak of development from single age or cross-sectional samples. Again, one answer is that the projected future work will provide the remedy. Further, when the studies are examined side by side, they can be seen to cover a broad span from the onset of adolescence to young adulthood. While the resulting horizontal picture is only tentative, it is also interesting and heuristic. This is important, because the field needs new ideas more than it needs elegant methodological designs at this time.

This is not the apology of a sympathetic reviewer. The authors do not need secondhand support. They have tried to break the mold in which most research on adolescence is done. They have been responsible in their effort by building from familiar referent points and seeking to go beyond them toward a new formulation that constrains adolescent development within the family context and that orients analysis of the family to the development of its members. As I will suggest later, this constitutes a significant forward step, since it allows the study of adolescence to be integrated with the study of other periods of development as well as with research by other social sciences.

Individuals and Relations

The chapters in this volume can be arranged along a scale that places the individual at one end and relations at the other. Powers, Hauser, Schwartz, Noam, and Jacobson represent the individualist approach through their version of structural-developmental theory. They focus on the adolescent's ego functioning, defined generally as self-managed activity through which the adolescent struggles to make sense of experience and to construct a stable view of reality and of the self within it. They recognize the social milieu in which ego development proceeds, and they treat it as the context that facilitates or impedes the adolescent's ego functioning and development.

Bell and Bell present a position that falls near the other end of the scale. They also assign responsibility to the individual adolescent, who must construct conceptions of other persons and of self. However, they view construction as social, insofar as the process of construction depends on engagement in interactive communication for the participants' validity. They add, moreover, that the process also involves mutual support, which is affective in basis and interpersonal in its constitution. They call this mutual support valuing and propose that it runs parallel to validations by providing the climate that enables coconstruction to occur.

White, Speisman, and Costos and Cooper, Grotevant, and Condon also partake of the individualistic and the rational approaches. However, both groups of authors are closer to Bell and Bell than they are to Powers and colleagues. For White and her colleagues, the focus is on the development of the parent-young adult relations, which is coterminous with the development of young adults as individuals. Cooper and her colleagues present a similar conceptualization, since they see the parent-adolescent relation as the supraordinate development within which the adolescent's individuation follows.

The notion that there is a developmental course to the parent-adolescent relation and the parent-young adult relation is not widespread in the literature. The more conventional view is that the adolescent develops as an individual precisely by moving outside the relation with parents. The conventional view also holds that this movement occurs through the adolescent's own efforts as he or she resorts to reasoning that is self-instigated and self-guided. The formulations offered in the present volume are clearly not conventional and merit further elaboration. To this end, I divide the argument into two parts, one pertaining to the structure of the parent-adolescent relation and one to the process of change.

The Parent-Adolescent Relation

One can hardly speak of adolescents without taking account of their relation with parents. A general proposition that supercedes theoretical differences has come to be an assumption in the field. This proposition holds that adolescents strive to become individuals who are self-defined, not ascribed definition by their parents. The idea has been expressed in a variety of ways. For example, psychoanalytic thinkers propose that adolescents must shift object relations from parents to nonparents in order to achieve genital maturity (Freud, 1968). Contemporary cognitive theorists state the point in terms of the adolescent's exchanging views based on conformity to parent's wishes for views autonomously constructed through reasoning.

Thus, direction has been imputed to development during the adolescent period. The presumption is that, at the onset of adolescence, young teenagers have identities formed in adaptation to years of living within the parent-child relation. To accept these identities and the views of reality attendant on that relation is to be immature. The path to maturity opens when adolescents step outside the relation and begin to adapt to society and persons with whom they will be living in the future.

It is noteworthy that theorists of the bent just outlined describe adolescents as breaking the hold of the parent-child bond by turning outside the relation. In psychoanalytic theory, adolescents turn to nonparental figures, who are other adults and peers. For cognitive theorists, the turn is inward to reasoning when the capacity for formal thinking gives adolescents a new basis for self-reliance. In summary, then, the individuality is posed in counterpoint both to the parent-child and to the parent-adolescent relation.

Let us now look closely at the ways in which the individual-relation tension is dealt with in the present volume. Cooper and colleagues present a clear articulation of the problem as well as a plausible synthesis. They pose a dialectic between rank individuality at one extreme and stultifying enmeshment in the parent-child relation at the other. The resolution is made through individuation, which allows the adolescent both to declare separateness from parents and distinctiveness from their ascriptions and to accept connectedness with parents.

Bell and Bell adopt virtually the same position but ground it in a different explanatory system. They propose that being an individual and being in relation with one's parents are not oppositional but represent two sides of a single whole. The adolescent needs the relation for individuality, because it is through this relation that the adolescent can hope to get validation for a conception of self. To abandon the relation is to risk giving up the known grounds for validation and a key criterial base for estimating personal worth.

White and colleagues carry the argument further with their focus on young adults in their mid twenties. For them, individuation in the sense defined by Cooper and colleagues begins during the adolescent period with regard to the parental relation. That relation is not given up but remains the point of focus as older adolescents take the next step when they begin to appreciate their parents, who in turn begin to adopt a new perspective on their offspring's point of view. A third step is then posited. Given what has preceded, young adults and their parents can begin to work together toward symmetry and mutuality through which they understand and treat each other as equals yet with respect for their individual personalities.

Reiss and colleagues provide a compatible but different approach that seeks a balance between the poles of individualism and enmeshment. Their typology for families brings out the balance. For example, consensus-sensitive families place a premium on seeking a common perspective at the expense of individual views. In contrast, environment-sensitive families collaborate in problem solving and yet promote autonomy in their adolescent members. A third type, the distance-sensitive family, seems to favor individuality but not collaboration. Thus, the middle type comes closest to fitting the reconciliation between giving up of self for the family and abandoning the family for self. That there is a middle ground is important, since the presumption is that one can find self through family membership.

The Primacy of Relationship

The construct of individuation within a continuing parent-offspring relation is an important and radical revision for psychological theories. The purpose of this section is to show its implications for theories of adolescence found in other social sciences—in particular, sociology and social history. Theorists from these other disciplines also have interests in the parent-adolescent relation, and the data that they have generated should bear on the parallel interests of psychologists. I suggest that the treatment of individuation just specified makes eventual integration among disciplines possible, which more conventional constructs, such as individuality, identity, and autonomy, do not.

The first point is drawn from recent studies in social history that have focused on historical changes in relations between parents or families and adolescents or youth. There is evidence that, in the late nineteenth century, it became commonplace for adolescents not to leave home and family at the onset of adolescence but to remain in residence with their parents in the family household (compare Gillis, 1981; Kett, 1977). At about the same time, the demographic structure of the family began to change. In the United States, the number of children per family declined by about half between 1800 and 1900, reaching approximately three by the latter date. Simultaneously, life expectancy for adults began to increase. It then became common for parents to live long enough to witness their offspring's adult lives. Consequently, adolescents and their parents could look forward to overlapping adult life spans (Degler, 1980).

It is obvious that these conditions, which emerged about 100 years ago, prevail today with minor variations. In the face of these facts, one might argue that there is an essential realism to individuation and to the proposal that the parent-offspring relation develops within the family during adolescence and with regard to the family thereafter. In contrast, alternative constructs that stress autonomy appear somewhat unreal. The realism comes from recognizing that the parent-adolescent relation remains extant throughout the period. Pragmatically speaking, it is reasonable to propose that coexistence in residence requires mutual adaptation on both sides. To suggest that the relation is rejected or abandoned is not to take cognizance of a basic material condition.

The construct of individuation fills a void that autonomy and its variants do not address. It leads to the proposal that adolescents and their parents seek a way to maintain their relation while each holds to the self's individuality. The fact that adolescence does not signal the end of coexistence meshes neatly with the idea that the forging of shared perspectives and mutuality constitutes further steps in the relation. In short, autonomy as abandonment of the relation falls outside the realm of sociological credibility. At the same time, the notion that the relation is transformed, not abandoned, and that it can be developed through adulthood puts psychological theory squarely into sociological reality.

Individualism and Family Solidarity

The foregoing argument is now carried forward, because the issue at stake goes beyond data to ideology. Within sociology, debate regarding the status of the individual in modern society continues. The focus has been Parson's view (Parsons and Bales, 1955) that the structure of society has shifted and that this shift has consequences for personality. Parsons argues that the structure of modern society is such that the adaptive personality is a composite of a complex of variables. They include definition of person through achievement, control of self through impersonal generalized rules, adoption of affect-neutral social judgments, forgoing of communal interests for individual ends, and dealing with persons according to specific ends.

Connections between the mature personality envisioned by Parsons and the mature individual presumed by conventional theories of adolescence are obvious. Removal of self from the parent-child relation in order to establish a personal identity is a Parsonian conception. It is reinforced by the proposition that individualness is created by the adolescent, who manages to make sense of input by relying on reasoning as the arbiter. The resulting autonomous person owes little if anything to the past, much less to the person's relationship with parents, which must be overcome and superseded.

There is strong evidence that Parsons's view is a misconstruction of both cause and effect. It represents a biased reading of structural change in society. The bias comes from an objectification of formal institutions and a failure to take account of institutions that do not fit the model, such as the family. Some social historians contest Parsons on this point and cite evidence that shows that family affiliations remained strong after the shift to modernity and after industrialization (compare Hareven, 1978; Scott and Tilly, 1979). While it is true that young persons left their families for work in distant geographical places, it was not necessarily the rule that they adopted individualistic personalities at the sacrifice of relations with their families.

More current evidence on the point is available from sociological researchers who have contested Parsons on basic descriptive grounds. They have looked at contemporary urban citizens, who should epitomize the results of Parsonian modernity and individualism. They have asked these persons with whom they have intimate relations, how important these relations are, how these relations are maintained, how much contact there is between participants, and so on. First, most adults, both men and women, claim to be members of intimate relations. Second, of the persons mentioned in these relations, parents and siblings rank consistently among the first choices. Third, contact is regular and occurs through multiple means varying from face-to-face visits to telephone calls. Fourth, persons say that they exchange personal information in these relations and that they keep up with affairs in each other's life. Fifth, persons perceive that they can rely on these intimates for advice, amusement, and help if they need it to overcome difficulties. Sixth, besides naming family members as intimates, many subjects designated as intimates friends whom they have known since childhood and youth (compare Fischer, 1977; Laumann, 1973; Wellman, 1979; Yanagisako, 1977).

The picture that emerges from these results is a logical extension of the findings noted by social historians. Adults maintain a sense of intimacy with their parents, siblings, and childhood friends throughout the life cycle. This does not contradict individuality but surely tempers it while giving material substance to the developmental sequence from individuation through mutuality. What remains to be explored are the dynamics that keep these relations functioning so that the persons involved can continue to steer a path between disengaged separateness and cloying enmeshment. The issue, of course, exceeds the bounds of our focus here, which is on the period from the teen years to the mid twenties.

Social Construction

The foregoing position on the development of interpersonal relations is closely associated with a second substantive theme in the studies described in this volume. The conventional perspective on individualism pertains to more than the putative product of development. It more often than not refers also to the hypothesized process by which development proceeds. What is meant by individualism in process is best represented by contemporary cognitive theories (compare Blasi, 1980; Sampson, 1981). The theorists in question presume that the impetus for development arises within the subject, who continually monitors concepts for purposes of maintaining internal equilibrium. Occasions for developmental action occur when concepts are found to be at odds or when a conception comes to be seen as disparate from the reality of some outer event.

According to this view, the brunt of development falls on the individual's self-reflective capacity, which consists in reconciling differences through the use of reasoning. It is the individual who discovers conflict or disparity. It is the individual who struggles to overcome disequilibrium. And, it is the individual who makes the reconciliation that brings disparate conceptions into line and that finds ways to match conceptions with outer reality. The emphasis here is on self-reliance, since the individual regularly turns to inward powers to keep an orderly posture of self toward objects and other persons.

What this position neglects — and what the chapters in this volume do not neglect — is the social side of the developmental process. The point can be made from a review of the two versions of role taking found in these chapters. One is based on the individualistic, self-reflecting adolescent, while the other is predicated on a process of coconstruction of views. The former, which is the conventional position of many cognitive theories, holds that role taking is a developmental phenomenon bound at one end by egocentrism and at the other, mature end by the capacity for recursive thinking about the dealings in which self and other are engaged. In summary, a first step out of egocentrism is made when the individual notices disparities between self's and other's views and recognizes that two persons can perceive, think, and feel differently about the same event. A further step is taken when the individual realizes that different viewpoints can be coordinated. For instance, the self can begin to appreciate the other's view by taking the other's position or recreating the steps by which the other reached that position. Still another step is taken when the self can assume a third party's or outsider's view of self and other. Finally, the self can reason "I think that you think that I think" in a recursive stream.

Why is there development in role taking? The conventional answer seems to be that the individual is compelled to break out of egocentrism and move toward mature stages because the individual senses disparity between self and other. The self then begins to question its own view and through reflection finds that, while it is correct, there may be other views. The continual return to reflection in the face of disparity leads the individual to appreciate self-other differences and eventually prods the self, first, to coordinate views, then, to gain distance from any particular view.

This version can be called the stone face theory of role taking to emphasize that the other has little influence on development. The other's major function is to serve as an occasion for disparity, which causes disequilibrium within the subject and forces the self toward internal reflective revision. The other is benign and apparently plays no part in making its view clear to the self. The other is equally impotent with respect to coordination, which depends solely on the self's capacity to make sense of difference. In short, the development of role taking as conventional theorists see it is self-initiated and self-achieved, although it is centered on the other.

A second view of role taking—the one represented by the preceding chapters—is grounded in a radically different process. It is a social and a communicative process. And, it is utterly more realistic than the stone face theory allows. Glimpses of its elements can be seen in the chapter by Powers and colleagues, who depict parents as the other and the adolescent as the self. In their study, parents are described not as passive others waiting to be understood but as agents who want to communicate their views to adolescent offspring. However, Powers and colleagues remain within the conventional model, because they assume that only the adolescent can construct the parent's views. For example, they stress that the parents' communication initiatives challenge the adolescent to revise his or her current way of understanding the social world. Challenge in this sense implies suggestion or invitation. Ultimately, then, it is up to the adolescent's own self-reflection to critique, test, and revise his or her own point of view.

Cooper and colleagues take a decisive step toward analyzing role taking as a process of social rather than individual construction. It is noteworthy that their classes of communicative acts apply equally to adolescents and parents and that their coding scheme is directed to communication behaviors that indicate individuality and connectedness in relationships. That is, roles, views, and perspectives are constructed by communicative enjoining of self and other. What, we may ask, is meant by social construction of role taking, and how does it differ from conventional theory?

The coding scheme of Cooper and colleagues contains numerous examples of the hypothesized coconstruction process. How does one person let the other know that the other and the one disagree? The one disagrees overtly, challenges the other's idea directly, or states a request, for example, "Wait a minute" or "Let's vote on it." What applies to the one in this scheme applies also to the other, since the code implies symmetry. How does the one communicate agreement with the other and vice versa? Again, there are several ways, including acknowledgment, agreement with, compliance with the other's request, and following the other's statement with a relevant, not an irrelevant, comment.

Perhaps the gist of social construction is made no more clearly than in the categories that Cooper and colleagues call designations of mutuality. The codes here explicitly refer to coconstruction of a common view through seeking compromise, suggesting action, stating other's feelings, answering requests, and validating. These codes explicitly refer to the coordination aspect of role taking. If we take them at face value, we see that coordination need not be construed as a self seeking to reconcile differences with another by groping with self-reflection. Instead of turning inward, an individual can step out toward the other and enter into communication so that differences can be discussed, questioned, and probed. When two persons do this, they can co-order respective views and coconstruct a mutually understood view.

Reiss and colleagues propose still another approach to the same issue. They view role taking as a social construction and suggest that role taking can proceed from the family to the adolescent or the reverse. Moreover, they insightfully propose that families can choose their own theoretical frame (role), which is constructed by members in interactions with one another and with the environment outside the family. The second point is important, since it brings in the third party not as an abstraction but in terms of society. This helps us to keep in mind that perspectives not only issue from persons in face-to-face exchange but involve perceptions of social others who bear on the interactants—in this case the paradigm held by family members of themselves.

Bell and Bell elaborate on coconstruction most pointedly in advancing their version of mutual validation. This concept has been used by social construction theorists to show the fallacy inherent in self-reflection (Cook-Gumperz and Corsaro, 1977; Macmurray, 1961; Piaget, 1932; Sullivan, 1953). They ask how a self-reliant thinker can know whether he or she is caught in self-deception. The answer, these theorists suggest, is by seeking validation outside the self. And, when this is done by two persons reciprocally, they should arrive at a view that has been honed on mutual criticism and clarification. When this mode of functioning is adopted, each individual acts as counterpoint to the other, so that reflection takes place in public and the view that each person holds is the result of mutual construction.

Although White and colleagues do not present data that denote social interactive construction, the process implied in development is virtually the same as that just noted. The keynote to their cooperation is dialogue in relationship as a result of which parents contribute as much as the young adult to development of the relation. Part of the process involves mutual regulation with respect for individual differences. Ultimately, at the hypothesized more mature levels of the relation, it is assumed that parents and young adults should behave toward each other as peers or friends who can talk out differences to produce mutual understanding although individual differences in views remain (Youniss, 1980).

Perhaps it is because the authors have chosen to view adolescents in communication that the theme of social construction is sounded so strongly. Survey, questionnaire, and single-subject interview data may be more conducive to thinking of the adolescent as a lone reflective organizer of reality. Whatever the case, the fact remains that the authors of these chapters have advanced a picture of social construction that is ordinarily missing from the literature on adolescence. This picture is in keeping with communication- and relation-based theories of infancy and childhood (compare Ainsworth, 1969; Hinde, 1979). It can only add to the field of adolescence, especially in abetting emerging views, such as those that deny the image of lonely struggle and promote the realistic view that parents, friends, and others want to be resources for the adolescent's development (for example, Ford, 1982).

Social Constitutionalism

There is no consensus among psychologists on how to relate society to the individual. Rather, there are multiple approaches, which range from determinism, on one side or the other, to unspecified interactionism. It was probably not the intention of the authors of the chapters in this volume to take a stand on this issue. Nevertheless, their work does address it in a pertinent way. In this section, I will argue that a common outlook can be deduced and that this outlook has important features that promise to break the long-standing impasse.

The approach builds on the two points just discussed: consideration of the individual in relationship and recognition of social construction as a development process. It follows that the agents of development include the adolescent and other persons, not the least of whom are parents. The specific means of developing is through interactive exchange, which I have already described as public reflection. The agents can be understood as going back and forth in turns, so that one serves to reflect the other's ideas or feeling, and then their roles are reversed. Rather than calling this a case of reciprocal influence, we can go further to conceive of the coconstruction process as one in which two agents cooperate to reach common understanding. The assumption is that the two may want both to be understood and to understand and therefore that they work together toward reaching consensus (Youniss, 1980, 1981).

The usual way of viewing communication in the literature on adolescence involves two individuals who come together to interact for some purpose. The chapters in this volume allow this general proposition to be redefined. First, the purpose, which can vary from one occasion to the next, is given an overall constancy, which is supraordinate to situational diversity. That purpose is mutual understanding, which at any moment can be more or less at the forefront but which is consistently in the background. Second, the matter of two individuals is recast in a developmental framework that brings society and individual together in a coherent manner.

Most of the authors conceive of the family as more than context or milieu. The distinction stems from the treatment of parent-adolescent interactions as constitutive of the relation and the individuals within it. That is to say, the relation becomes structured through interactions, so the individuals are structured by the relation. Since the relation develops, so may the individuals who participate in it. If, as White and colleagues propose, the relation is marked by a high degree of asymmetry early in adolescence, it follows that the individuals could be distinguished at that time by the greater agency on the parents' part and by the greater passivity and complementariness on the adolescent's part. When this relation later evolves into mutuality, the participants would change correspondingly into equally potent individuals.

This view can be appreciated in light of the criticism that psychological theories too often tend toward abstraction, which lies at the heart of the separation between society and individual (compare Jacoby, 1975; Riegel, 1976). What this means is that the individual is abstracted from society and indeed any material context and treated as if he or she were an entity that developed of its own accord. Such an account allows development to proceed along a programmed course. All that is left for society is to help or impede the inevitable course.

The family can also be an abstraction, insofar as it denotes, in a particular fashion, society. For example, psychologists who study childrearing practices often treat practices as if parents voluntarily and rationally decided to employ them. The counterview considers the family as based on material conditions and the relations among family members as constituted through the relation of the family to society (for example, Lasch, 1977; Zaretsky, 1976). It is, of course, not the business of psychologists to analyze the family-society relation. Yet, it is in their interest to take cognizance of others' analyses and bring them to their own work.

The present authors do this to the degree that they treat the family not as an abstraction but as a system and to the degree that they examine the interactions by which that system functions. In keeping with avoidance of abstraction, the authors further break the term parents down into the persons of mother and father. In this vein, they permit differences to emerge that help us to see the family-society relation in an interesting way. The point merits further commentary.

Those concerned with the family-society relation agree that modern social structure has divided the roles so that mothers bear the brunt of childcare and childrearing. The studies in this volume are probably seeing the long-term effects of this role division, since by adolescence mothers have invested much in the relation with their offspring. Further, one can presume that the mother-adolescent relation has achieved a high degree of mutual understanding. It follows, finally, that the mother-adolescent and the father-adolescent relation have distinctive structures, not of necessity but through their respective interactive histories.

While it is not possible to compare results across studies in an exact way due to age differences among samples and to diversity of scoring schemes, two general points can be made. In each study, correlations were performed separately for mothers and fathers with respect to measures of adolescents' development. First, overall, there are more significant correlations between mothers and adolescents than there are between fathers and adolescents. Second, mothers appear to be more diverse and pervasive in these correlations, because what they do has either positive or negative effects. Fathers are not so diverse. Frequently, when their behavior correlates, it does so on a dimension for which the mothers' behavior is equally effective. The mother-father difference is supported in an interesting way by the finding of Cooper and colleagues that disagreement among parents correlates positively with adolescent's level of identity exploration.

Reiss and colleagues make the point in a different way. Their work on the concept of a family paradigm represent the core of social constitutionalism. Families have material social histories that give them a cohesive self-perception and an outlook on society. The idea is congruent with the position of social historians that families evolve strategies for subsistence and success when they confront material conditions and attempt to deal with them. Reiss and colleagues add that, in forming a definition of itself, the family affects the individual definitions of adolescent offspring. Moreover, as the adolescents themselves interact in society, they bring new data to the family's definition, and those data can reinforce a paradigm or cause it to be revised.

Again, it is not so much the results that are crucial at this time in these research programs as it is the general theoretical advance that these programs embody. The authors could have approached the family as mere context and treated it as background to the adolescent's inner development. Instead they imply that the adolescent becomes an individual through interactions with other family members. Indeed, for Reiss and colleagues the family is coconstructed with society at large. The developmental implication is that social process constitutes both the individual and his or her development.

This approach might well serve as a model for future research. It clearly avoids sociological reductionism, either through absorption of the individual by society or vice versa. It deals with society in an acceptable psychological manner; that is, it studies society through the unit of interpersonal relationship and through systems. Yet, the agency of the adolescent is fully possible in this unit. Last, the approach does not do away with individual self-reflection. Instead, it tempers self-reflection, in that it is brought to the public forum, where it meets resistance that would be avoided if the adolescent were allowed to turn inward.

Psychology and Sociology

The final tension with which I will deal is not found in the chapters but derived from them thematically. Adelson and Doehrman (1980) have noted that psychological and sociological theories offer quite different depictions of adolescence. For many psychologists, adolescence is a natural course of development that results from internal physiological upheaval and untamed new powers of cognition. In contrast, for many sociologists, adolescence is a product of society, whose structure cannot easily absorb physically mature persons who have completed childhood but who have yet to be assimilated into productive institutions.

There are two interpretations of the sociological perspective. One is reductionist, in the sense that adolescence becomes explicable through society's objective structure. For example, it could be argued that modern adolescence took shape when industrialized labor advanced to the point where institutions of employment were unable to assimilate young and potential workers. Society then needed to find substitute activities to fill the time of youth until they could become employed in society's major task of gainful work. Creation of compulsory high school education and later college enrollment can be seen as two strategies that answered the problem. These institutions not only substitute for wage earning, they are rationalized as means for enhancing wage earning once it is permitted to begin.

This form of sociological reductionism eliminates the need for an individual, since external forces and circumstances ultimately determine how persons shall be sorted out. It is important, therefore, that there is a second sociological perspective that is not reductionist and that allows room for the individual. This viewpoint partakes of social constructionism and rests on the proposition that society is divided into two sectors. The objective sector is comprised of systems that are lawful and impersonal in design. Economics is one such structure; it is run by generalized rules, which apply to all irrespective of individual characteristics. This side of society is well described by Parsons's theory of modern social structure.

The other sector, which has already been glimpsed in the discussion of interpersonal relations, is the part of society that relies on and arises from the social constructions of persons acting together. Habermas (1979), who calls this the *life world*, defines its structure in terms of intersubjectivity and calls its motive mutual understanding. This part of society is fostered by persons for their mutual well-being, and it penetrates objective social systems as much as they affect it. The life world has its own interest, which is as primary as that ordinarily assigned to economics. Persons maintain it because mutual understanding and solidarity are fundamental to existence.

As Gillis (1981) has noted, sociologists and social historians often think of society as an objective whole in the vein that Parsons and other functionalists prescribed. But, Gillis suggests that the historical data on youth do not sustain that position. Rather, says Gillis (1981, p. 219), the evidence shows that young people have a hand in the social construction of youth: "Each generation redefines its traditions to meet its particular needs." "Youth cultures... are not the product of material conditions alone" (p. 218). Youths perceive and act on society, and thus they help to create the circumstances in which they live. Moreover, they do this in continuity with their elders, with whom they "share a common heritage... that binds together the generations in common outlook and behavior" (p. 219).

It is not inconceivable that parents and adolescents are drawn together in part to confront the objective sector in a task that several social historians have termed *strategies for success* (compare Katz, 1981; Kett, 1977). While the historical evidence is new, the idea is not. Davis (1940) and Riesman (1953) articulated the point and showed its relevance for psychology through their analyses of historical shifts in parents' childrearing practices. In the view of these authors, parents have an interest in the social success of their offspring. Their practices are not determined by social structure but are constructed in order to help them and their offspring to operate within it.

Few psychologists have taken the opportunity to work out this non-reductionist sociology and exploit its potential lines of integration with psychology. One of the few is Furth (1983), who adds the developmental dimension that is missing from these enlightened sociological theories. As Furth views the issue, intersubjectivity is coconstructed and essential to the individual from infancy. From the onset, the individual is a person in relationship with others. This introduction to the life world of mutual understanding is continually renewed, not just through the parent-offspring relation but through relations outside, such as friendships (Youniss, 1980). Mutual support is built into the individual constitutively through intersubjectivity.

What the studies in this volume reinforce is that social construction for the sake of consensus continues through adolescence and that this social construction has been neglected in the study of parent-adolescent relations. It is to the authors' credit that they maintain this possibility while recognizing that the relation undergoes a transformation at the same time. The form of intersubjectivity that is evident at the onset of adolescence differs from the form of intersubjectivity found about ten years later. The young adult has established an individuated self that the early adolescent has not envisioned. At the same time, however, the young adult, who prizes the self's distinctiveness, also begins to appreciate the individuated character of the parents. Neither part of this balanced view arises de novo. Indeed, the balancing and the differentiated parts owe much to the communicative interaction that has gone on in the parent-adolescent relation and that sustains it through its transformation during the period.

Reiss and colleagues add an important dimension to this overall issue. Families have histories and outlooks which act as constraints on family members. Each style or type of family can warp communication and thereby affect its members, one to another, and more sustainingly in effects that fall to individuals. This point should not be overlooked as one of the central entailments of enjoining psychology with sociology. The advantage of conventional psychological theories is that the individual taken abstractly out of society or relations can be described as an internally balanced self in an ordered society. When we bring in relations, family systems, and society, we increase the opportunity for imbalance and tension and thus for disequilibrium. In admitting this possibility, the authors of the present chapters depart sharply from the conventional approach and open the door to a realism that the psychological study of adolescence sorely needs.

108

References

Adelson, J., and Doehrman, M. J. "The Psychodynamic Approach to Adolescence." In J. Adelson (Ed.), *Handbook of Adolescent Psychology.* New York: Wiley, 1980.

Ainsworth, M. D. S. "Object Relations, Dependency, and Attachment." *Child Development,* 1969, *40,* 969-1025.

Blasi, A. "Bridging Moral Cognition and Moral Action: A Critical Review of the Literature." *Psychological Bulletin,* 1980, *88,* 1-45.

Cook-Gumperz, J., and Corsaro, W. A. "Social-Ecological Constraints on Children's Communication Strategies." *Sociology,* 1977, *11,* 411-434.

Davis, K. "The Sociology of Parent-Youth Conflict." *American Sociological Review,* 1940, *5,* 523-535.

Degler, C. *At Odds.* New York: Oxford University Press, 1980.

Fischer, C. S. *Networks and Places: Relations in the Urban Setting.* New York: Free Press, 1977.

Ford, M. "Social Cognition and Social Competence in Adolescence." *Developmental Psychology,* 1982, *18,* 323-339.

Freud, A. "Adolescence." In A. E. Winder and D. L. Angus (Eds.), *Adolescence.* New York: American Book Company, 1968.

Furth, H. G. "Freud, Piaget, and Macmurray: A Theory of Knowledge from the Standpoint of Personal Relations." *New Ideas in Psychology,* 1983, *1,* 51-65.

Gillis, J. R. *Youth and History.* New York: Academic Press, 1981.

Gottman, J. M., and Ringland, J. T. "The Analysis of Dominance and Bidirectionality in Social Development." *Child Development,* 1981, *52,* 393-412.

Habermas, J. *Communication and the Evolution of Society.* Boston: Beacon Press, 1979.

Hareven, T. K. *Transitions: The Family and the Life Course in Historical Perspective.* New York: Academic Press, 1978.

Hinde, R. A. *Towards Understanding Relationships.* London: Academic Press, 1979.

Jacoby, R. *Social Amnesia.* Boston: Beacon Press, 1975.

Katz, M. B. "Social Class in North American Urban History." *The Journal of Interdisciplinary History,* 1981, *11,* 579-605.

Kett, J. F. *Rites of Passage.* New York: Basic Books, 1977.

Lasch, C. *Haven in a Heartless World.* New York: Basic Books, 1977.

Laumann, E. O. *Bonds of Pluralism.* New York: Wiley, 1973.

Macmurray, J. *Persons in Relation.* London: Faber & Faber, 1961.

Parsons, T., and Bales, R. F. *Family, Socialization, and Interaction Process.* Glencoe, Ill.: Free Press, 1955.

Piaget, J. *The Moral Judgment of the Child.* London: Routledge & Kegan Paul, 1932.

Riegel, K. F. "The Dialectics of Human Development." *American Psychologist,* 1976, *31,* 689-700.

Riesman, D. *The Lonely Crowd.* Garden City, N.Y.: Doubleday, 1953.

Sampson, E. E. "Cognitive Psychology as Ideology." *American Psychologist,* 1981, *36,* 730-743.

Scott, J. W., and Tilly, L. A. "Women's Work and the Family in Nineteenth-Century Europe." *Comparative Studies in Society and History,* 1979, *17,* 36-64.

Sullivan, H. S. *The Interpersonal Theory of Psychiatry.* New York: Norton, 1953.

Wellman, B. "The Community Question: The Intimate Network of East Yorkers." *American Journal of Sociology,* 1979, *84,* 1201-1231.

Yanagisako, S. J. "Women-Centered Kin Networks in Urban Bilateral Kinship." *American Ethnologist,* 1977, *44,* 207-226.

Youniss, J. *Parents and Peers in Social Development.* Chicago: University of Chicago Press, 1980.

Youniss, J. "Moral Development Through a Theory of Social Construction." *Merrill-Palmer Quarterly,* 1981, *27,* 385–403.

Zaretsky, E. *Capitalism, the Family, and Personal Life.* New York: Harper, 1976.

James Youniss is professor of psychology at Boys Town Center for the Study of Youth Development, Catholic University of America, Washington, D.C. His recent work concerns social relations in childhood and adolescence.

Index

A

Accurate interpersonal perception, and individuation, 29, 30, 32, 33, 34, 35, 36, 37, 39, 40

Adams, G. R., 85, 90

Adelson, J., 65, 75, 105, 108

Adolescent and Family Development Study, 6-23

Adolescent development: and developmental level, 1-2; and direction of effects, 2; down-from-society approach to, 77, 78-79, 82-85; and experience of adolescents in families, 3; and family interaction, 5-25; and family paradigms, 77-92; and family solidarity, 98-99; general comments on, 94-95; in identity formation and role taking, 43-59; individuals and relations in, 95-96; and individuation, 2, 27-42; issues in, 1-3; parent-adolescent relation in, 96-97; and parental validation and support, 27-42; primacy of relationship in, 97-98; psychological and sociological approaches to, 105-107; and psychopathology, 21-22; and research methodology, 2-3; and social constitutionalism, 103-105; and social construction, 93-109; up-from-adolescence approach to, 77-78, 79, 86

Adults, young: analysis of relationships of, with parents, 61-76; background on development of, 61-66; discussion of, 73-75; ego development of, 65, 69-70, 72-73; ethical and cognitive development of, 63-64; findings on, 71-73; and individuation, 63, 64-65, 68, 70; measures of, 67-71; method of studying, 66-71; and mutuality, 64-65, 68; perspective taking by, 64-65, 68, 69-70; procedures for, 71; psychosocial development of, 65, 70, 74; sample characteristics of, 66-67; sex differences among, 65-66, 73-75;

and social status, 66, 74; socialization experiences of, 74-75

Affect, and ego development, 10, 12, 21

Affective conflict, and ego development, 12, 13, 16, 17, 18-19, 21, 22

Ainsworth, M. D. S., 52, 56, 102, 108

Aldens, J., 75

American Diabetes Foundation, 5n

American Psychiatric Association, 11, 21-22, 23

Avoidance, and ego development, 12, 13, 16, 17, 18

Ayers-Lopez, S., 43n

B

Bales, R. F., 98, 108

Beardslee, W., 5n, 6, 23

Beavers, W. R., 44, 56, 57

Bell, D. C., 1, 2, 20, 27-42, 95, 96, 102

Bell, L. G., 1, 2, 20, 27-42, 95, 96, 102

Belsky, J., 44, 56

Bengston, V. L., 62, 66, 75

Bent, D. H., 58

Berger, P. L., 78, 90

Berkman, H., 91, 92

Berkowitz, M. W., 12, 23

Beukema, S., 5n

Bion, W., 80, 91

Black, K. D., 62, 66, 75

Blasi, A., 10, 23, 108

Block, J. H., 65, 75

Blos, P., 44, 48, 56

Boszormenyi-Nagy, I., 29, 41

Botkin, P. T., 57, 91

Bowen, M., 29, 41

Broderick, C. J., 44, 56

C

California Personality Inventory, 87

California Psychological Inventory (CPI), 32

Candee, D., 23

Carlson, R., 75

Chandler, M. J., 85, 91

Clark, R. A., 46, 56
Cognitive stimulation, and ego development, 7, 10, 12-13, 15-16
Colby, A., 11, 23
Coleman, J. C., 44, 56
Comfort with differences, and individuation and validation, 29, 32, 33, 34, 35, 37, 39, 40
Communication. *See* Family communication
Competitive challenging, and ego development, 12, 16, 17, 18, 21
Condon, S. , 1, 2, 3, 43-59, 63, 95
Configuration, in family paradigm, 80-81, 88, 89
Connectedness, and identity formation and role taking, 43-59
Cook-Gumperz, J., 102, 108
Cooper, C. R., 1-4, 43-59, 63, 95, 96, 97, 101, 105
Coordination, in family paradigm, 81, 88, 89, 90
Cornwell, C. S., 27n, 34, 41
Corsaro, W. A., 102, 108
Costell, R., 82, 83, 84, 90, 91, 92
Costos, D., 1, 2, 3, 61-76, 95
Coulthard, M., 49, 56
Cox, R. O., 62, 75
Curd, K., 1, 3, 77-92

D

Daffner, K., 5n
Davis, K., 107, 108
Davis, P., 82, 91
Day, J., 24, 42, 92
Degler, C., 98, 108
Delia, J. G., 46, 56
Derman, D., 57
Developmental Environments Coding System (DECS), 12, 13, 21
Differentiated self-awareness, and individuation, 29, 32, 33, 34, 37
Distortion, and ego development, 12, 13, 16, 17, 18
Doehrman, M. J., 105, 108
Dore, J., 49, 57
Douvan, E., 65, 75
Duncan, O. D., 14, 23
Duncan Socioeconomic Index, 14
Durrett, M. E., 44, 57
Dymond, R., 87, 88, 89, 91

E

Eckman, G. A., 39, 41
Ego development: and accurate interpersonal perception, 36, 39, 40; and adolescent behavior, 20; analysis of, 5-25; assessments of, 12-14; and background variables, 14; and cognitive stimulation, 7, 10, 12-13, 15-16; conclusions on, 20-23; of family members, 14-15; interference with, 12, 13; longitudinal analyses needed for, 22-23; method of studying, 10-14; milestones of, 8-9; and parental behavior, 15-20; procedures for studying, 11-12; results of study of, 14-20; sample for, 10-11; structural-developmental approach to, 7, 10; theory of, 6-7; of young adults, 65, 69-70, 72-73
Ego Identity Interview, 49, 50
Ego Identity Status Interview, 67
Eisenberg-Berg, N., 85, 91
Ekstrom, R. B., 51, 57
Empathy: as component: 85-86; and family paradigm, 85-90; findings on, 88-89; measures of, 87-88; sample for study of, 87; sex differences in, 88-90
Erickson, L. V., 10, 23
Erickson, E. H., 46, 50, 53, 57, 65, 70, 75
Everett, B., 46, 58
Extended Range Vocabulary Test, 49, 51

F

Family communication: analysis of, 43-59; background on, 43-45; conclusions on, 55-56; discussion of, 51-55; method of studying, 49-51; procedures in study of, 49-51; qualitative findings on, 54-55; subjects in study of, 49
Family Environment Scale, 32
Family interaction: analysis of, 5-25; background on, 5-6; conclusions on, 20-23; results of study of, 14-20; structural-developmental approach to, 7, 10
Family Interaction Task (FIT), 49-50, 51

Family paradigm: achievement-sensitive, 81, 83, 84; and adolescent social behavior, 77–92; background on, 77–79; and boundary issues, 82–83; closure in, 81; configuration in, 80–81, 88, 89; consensus-sensitive, 81, 83, 97; coordination in, 81, 88, 89, 90; and cycle hypothesis, 84–85; distance-sensitive, 81, 83, 84, 85, 88, 97; and down-from-society approach, 82–85; and empathy, 85–90; and engagement issues, 82–83; environment-sensitive, 81, 83, 84, 85, 86, 88, 97; and problem solving, 80–82; and social transactions, 79–82

Family Relationships Interview (FRI), 65, 67–69, 71, 72

Family relationships stage: concept of, 66; and ego development, 72–73

Family systems theory: and communication, 44, 45–46; and validation and support, 28, 40

Faunce, E. E., 31, 42, 45, 58

Feffer, M. H., 48, 50, 51, 57, 85, 91

Feiring, C., 44, 57

Feldman, L., 32, 34, 41

Fischer, C. S., 99, 108

Flavell, J. H., 48, 57, 85, 91

Focusing, and ego development, 12, 17, 18

Follansbee, D. J., 23, 91

Foote, N., 75

Ford, M., 103, 108

French, J. W., 57

Freud, A., 96, 108

Fry, C. L., 57, 87, 88, 89, 91

Furth, H. G., 107, 108

G

Gallatin, J., 70, 75

Gibbs, J. C., 12, 23

Gilligan, C., 88, 90, 91

Gillis, J. R., 97, 106, 108

Gonzales, S., 92

Gossett, J. T., 57

Gottman, J. M., 94, 108

Gould, R. L., 62, 75

Gourevitch, S., 48, 57, 85, 91

Gregg, T., 43n

Grossier, D., 5n

Grotevant, H. D., 1–4, 43–59, 63, 95

H

Habermas, J., 106, 108

Handel, G., 80, 91

Hareven, T. K., 99, 108

Harman, H. H., 57

Hartup, W. W., 44, 57

Harvard Medical School, Adolescent and Family Development Study of, 6–23

Hauser, S. T., 1, 5–25, 69, 75, 78, 91, 95

Hazen, N. L., 44, 57

Heilbrun, P. G., 43n

Henley, N., 87, 91

Hess, R. D., 80, 91

Hewer, A., 23

Hill, J. P., 44, 46, 48, 57

Hill, R., 44, 57, 66, 75

Hinde, R. A., 64, 75, 102, 108

Hirsch, S., 24, 42

Hoeffner, T., 43n

Hoffman, M. L., 88, 91

Hogan, R., 87, 88, 89, 91

Hogg Foundation for Mental Health, 43n

Hollingshead, A. B., 14, 23

Hollingshead Educational Scale, 14

Hollingshead-Redlich scale, 87

Holt, R. R., 14, 24

Houlihan, J., 61n, 76

Howard, K. I., 58

Huber, C., 5n

Hughes, A. S., 91

Hull, C. H., 58

Huston, T. L., 45, 57

I

Identity formation: as developmental task, 46, 48–49; and individuality and connectedness, 43–59; results of study of, 51–53

Imbasciati, C., 61n, 76

Individualism, and family solidarity, 98–99

Individuality, and identity formation and role taking, 43–59

Individuation: analysis of, 27–42; concepts of, 2; discussion of, 40–41; in family systems, 45–46; and parent-adolescent relation, 97–98; process of,

Individuation *(continued)*
28–30, 31; results of study of, 35–40; theoretical model and method for, 32–35; validation related to, 29, 30, 33, 37, 39–40; of young adults, 63, 64–65, 68, 70
Interaction. *See* Family interaction
Interaction Process Coding Scheme, 34
Intimacy Interview, 67

J

Jacobson, A., 1, 5–25, 91, 95
Jacoby, R., 104, 108
Jarvis, R. W., 57, 91
Jenkins, J. G., 58
Jenson, G. O., 90
Johnson, J., 5n
Johnson, S. C., 16, 24
Jones, C., 91, 92
Jöreskog, K., 35, 41
Jorgenson, J., 91
Jorgenson, S. R., 75
Joslin Diabetes Center Biomedical Research Support Program and DRTC, 5n

K

Kafka, J. S., 76
Karpel, M., 64, 75
Kasendorf, E., 5n
Katz, M. B., 106, 108
Katz, R., 85, 91
Kegan, R., 6, 24
Keniston, K., 62–63, 64, 75
Kett, J. F., 97, 106, 108
Klein, D. M., 62, 75
Klein, M. M., 82, 92
Kluckhohn, F. R., 80, 91
Koch, G. C., 13, 24
Kohlberg, L., 5n, 6, 11, 23, 24
Koran, L. M., 83, 91
Kramer, N., 92
Kuhn, T. S., 79–80, 91

L

Laing, R. L., 29, 41
Lamb, L., 43n
Landis, J. R., 13, 24
Lasch, C., 104, 108

Laumann, E. O., 99, 108
Lerner, R. M., 44, 57
Levinger, G., 65–66, 76
Levinson, D. J., 63, 76
Lewis, J. M., 44, 45, 57
Lieberman, A. F., 44, 57
Liese, K., 5n
Linton, R., 78, 91
Loevinger, J., 6–7, 9n, 10, 14, 22, 24, 29, 32, 34, 41, 65, 69, 70, 71, 72, 73, 76, 78
Luckmann, T., 78, 90

M

MacArthur Foundation, 5n
Macdonald, R., 75
Macmurray, J., 102, 108
Marcia, J. E., 46, 50, 58, 65, 67, 76
Maternal and Child Health Research Grant Program, 5n
Matteson, D. R., 65, 76
Mead, G. H., 78, 92
Meyer, M. L., 43n, 57
Miller, B. C., 75
Minnesota Multiphasic Personality Inventory (MMPI), 87
Minuchin, S., 29, 42, 44, 45, 58
Mishler, E. G., 31, 42
Moore, M. S., 56
Moos, R. H., 32, 42
Moral Judgment Interview, 11
Mussen, P., 85, 91
Mutuality: and identity formation and role taking, 46, 47, 51, 55, 56; and social construction, 101–102; and young adults, 64–65, 68

N

National Institute of Child Health and Human Development, 43n
National Institute of Mental Health, 5n, 27n, 61
Newman, B. M., 63, 66, 76
Newman, P. R., 63, 66, 76
Nie, N. H., 50, 58
Noam, G., 1, 5–25, 91, 95
Noncompetitive sharing of perspectives, and ego development, 12, 16, 17, 18, 21
Nye, F. I., 78, 92

O

Offer, D., 44, 58
Oliveri, M. E., 1, 3, 77–92
Olson, D. H., 44, 45, 58, 76
Orlofsky's Intimacy Interview, 67
Ostrov, E., 58
Ozer, D., 61n

P

Palmquist, W. H., 46, 48, 57
Parents: and ego development, 15–20; and sex differences, 104–105
Parsons, T., 98, 99, 106, 108
Permeability, and identity formation and role taking, 46, 47, 51–52, 53, 55, 56
Perspective taking, by young adults, 64–65, 68, 69–70
Perspective-Taking Interview, 67
Phelps, E., 5n
Phillips, V. A., 57
Piaget, J., 6, 24, 102, 108
Positive receptive attitude, and validation, 30–31, 33, 34, 35, 37, 38–39, 40
Positive self-regard, and validation, 30–31, 32, 33, 34, 37, 38–39, 40
Power, C., 23
Powers, S. I., 1, 5–25, 91, 95, 101
Psychosocial development, of young adults, 65, 70, 74
Putnam, B., 5n

R

Raabe, V. L., 91
Rausch, H. L., 65–66, 76
Redmore, C., 24
Reiss, D., 1, 3, 77–92, 97, 102, 105, 107
Rejection of task, and ego development, 12, 13, 16, 17, 18
Relationship, primacy of, 97–98
Riegel, K. F., 104, 108
Riesman, D., 107, 108
Ringland, J. T., 94, 108
Riskin, J., 31, 42, 45, 58
Robins, E., 45, 57
Role taking: as developmental task, 46, 48–49; and individuality and connectedness, 43–59; results of study of, 53–54; and social construction, 100–102

Role-Taking Task (RTT), 49, 50–51
Rubin, K. H., 46, 58
Russell, C. S., 58
Ryckoff, I. M., 24, 42, 92
Ryder, R. G., 66, 76

S

Salzman, C., 82, 92
Sameroff, A. J., 44, 58
Sampson, E. E., 108
Schvaneveldt, J. D., 90
Schwartz, J. M., 1, 5–25, 95
Scott, J. W., 99, 108
Self-assertion, and identity formation and role taking, 45–46, 47, 52, 53, 55
Selman, R. L., 6, 24, 46, 48, 58, 67
Separateness, and identity formation and role taking, 46, 47–48, 51, 53, 55
Sex differences: in childrearing, 104–105; in empathy, 88–90; among young adults, 65–66, 73–75
Seymer, L., 43n
Shantz, C. U., 46, 58
Shulman, S., 82, 92
Skynner, A. C. R., 29, 42
Smith, J., 44, 56
Sociability, of adolescents, 82–85
Social behavior: and ego development, 20; and family paradigm, 77–92
Social constitutionalism, and adolescent development, 103–105
Social construction: of adolescence, 93–109; analysis of, 99–103; and parent-adolescent relations, 107
Soderquist, L., 43n
Sorbom, D., 35, 41
Spanier, G. B., 44, 57
Speicher-Dubin, B., 23
Speisman, J. C., 1, 2, 3, 61–76, 95
Speisman Part-Conflicts Scale (SPCS), 70, 71, 72
Spencer Foundation, 5n
Sprenkle, D. H., 58
Sroufe, L. A., 58
Steier, F., 91
Steinbrenner, K., 58
Steinglass, P., 92
Stern, D., 91
Stone, C. R., 46, 58
Strodtbeck, F. L., 11, 24, 80, 91

Structural-developmental approach, and ego development, 7, 10
Suchotliff, L., 50, 57
Sullivan, H. S., 6, 24, 102, 108
Support: and ego development, 12, 15–16, 17, 21, 22; and validation, 30–31, 33, 34, 37, 38–39, 40
Sussman, M. B., 66, 76

T

Temple, J., 5n
Texas at Austin, University of, 43n
Thorbecke, W. L., 57
Tilly, L. A., 99, 108
Turner, B., 5n
Turner, R. H., 48, 58

V

Validation: analysis of, 27–42; discussion of, 40–41; and individuation, 29, 30, 33, 37, 39–40; process of, 30–31; results of study of, 35–40; and social construction, 102; theoretical model and method for, 32–35

W

Walsh, F., 45, 58
Washington University Sentence Completion Test (WUSCT), 14, 69–70, 71
Waters, E., 44, 58
Waxler, N. E., 31, 42
Weinstein, E., 85, 92
Weiss, B., 23, 91
Wellman, B., 99, 108
Wessler, R., 6, 9n, 14, 24, 32, 41
White, K. M., 1, 2, 3, 61–76, 95, 97, 102, 103
Wippman, J., 58
Wolin, S., 92
Wright, J. W., 57, 91
Wynne, L. C., 18, 24, 29, 42, 80, 92

Y

Yanagisako, S. J., 99, 108
Youniss, J., 3, 93–109
Yussen, S. R., 48, 58

Z

Zaretsky, E., 104, 109

Statement of Ownership , Management, and Circulation
(Required by 39 U.S.C. 3685)

1. Title of Publication: New Directions for Child Development. A. Publication number: 494-090. 2. Date of filing: 9/30/83. 3. Frequency of issue: quarterly. A. Number of issues published annually: four. B. Annual subscription price: $35 institutions; $21 individuals. 4. Location of known office of publication: 433 California Street, San Francisco (San Francisco County), California 94104. 5. Location of the headquarters or general business offices of the publishers: 433 California Street, San Francisco (San Francisco County), California 94104. 6. Names and addresses of publisher, editor, and managing editor: publisher—Jossey-Bass Inc., Publishers, 433 California Street, San Francisco, California 94104; editor—William Damon, Department of Psychology, Clark University, Worcester, Mass. 01610; managing editor—William E. Henry, 433 California Street, San Francisco, California 94104. 7.Owner: Jossey-Bass Inc., Publishers, 433 California Street, San Francisco, California 94104. 8. Known bondholders, mortgages, and other security holders owning or holding 1 percent or more of total amount of bonds, mortgages, or other securities: same as No. 7. 10. Extent and nature of circulation: (Note: first number indicates average number of copies of each issue during the preceding 12 months; the second number indicates the actual number of copies published nearest to filing date.) A. Total number of copies printed (net press run): 1589, 1605. B. Paid circulation, 1) Sales through dealers and carriers, street vendors, and counter sales: 85, 40. 2) Mail subscriptions: 512, 512. C. Total paid circulation: 597, 552. D. Free distribution by mail, carrier, or other means (samples, complimentary, and other free copies): 125, 125. E. Total distribution (sum of C and D): 722, 677. F. Copies not distributed, 1) Office use, left over, unaccounted, spoiled after printing: 867, 928. 2) Returns from news agents: 0, 0. G. Total (sum of E, F1, and 2—should equal net press run shown in A): 1589, 1605. I certify that the statements made by me above are correct and complete.

JOHN R. WARD
Vice-President